the St. Louis Wedding Book

The St. Louis Wedding Book
Two Sisters' Guide to Your Ultimate Wedding

by Emily Ayala & Allison Hockett

ISBN: 978-0-615-34346-4

Printed in the United States of America

Copyright © 2010 by Emily Ayala & Allison Hockett

All rights reserved. No parts of this book may be reproduced or transmitted in any form or by any means, electronic or mechanical, including photocopying, recording or by any information storage and retrieval system, without written permission from the author, except for the inclusion of brief quotations in a review.

Wright Publications, LLC
6311 Ronald Reagan Dr. Suite 175
Lake St. Louis, MO 63367

www.stlweddingbook.com

the St. Louis Wedding Book

Two Sisters' Guide to Your Ultimate Wedding

Emily Ayala and Allison Hockett

Wright Publications

In memory of our dad, Larry Creager;
Gone but never forgotten.
Our hearts will always be with the greatest dad
we could have ever asked for.
You lived your life for us
and now we'll live ours to honor you.
We love and miss you.

— *Your Girls*

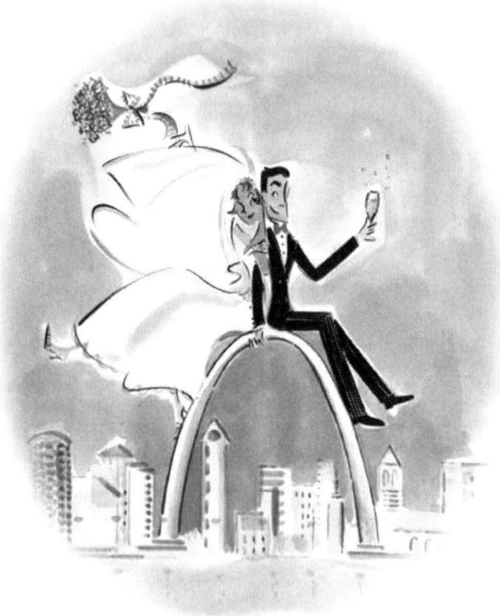

Contents

Acknowledgments

Introduction 1

Planning Timeline 3

1. Ceremonies and Officiants 5
2. Receptions 19
3. Catering 45
4. Music 55
5. Photography 65
6. Videography 77
7. Flowers 85
8. Cakes 93
9. Transportation 105
10. Stationery 113
11. Dresses 123
12. Tuxedos 133
13. And Everything Else 139

About Us 147

Resources at a Glance 149

Acknowledgments

We would like to thank all of the people whose tireless efforts and contributions made this book possible:

Our husbands, Brian and Paulo, for their complete support and hours of watching the kids so that we could finish this project.

Our children, Grace, Claire, Sam, and Adam, for keeping their sweet smiles while Mommy was busy working on her book.

Our mom, Karen Creager, for always believing in us, supporting our ideas, and providing hours of babysitting.

Our grandma, Frances Wright, for always encouraging us to finish despite all of the obstacles.

Ann Seebeck, author of *Favorite Places to Go with Kids in St. Louis*, and Marcie Bronowicz, coauthor of *Girlfriends on the Go*, for all the ideas and helpful hints on publishing.

Katherine Hinkebein, our editor.   www.popediting.net

Sue Sylvia, our book designer.   www.staircasepressdesign.com

Sharon Watts, our cover illustrator.   www.sharonwatts.com

All of our friends and family that gave us referrals, suggestions, and ideas for this book.

Brian and Allison Hockett
August, 11, 2001

Paulo and Emily Ayala
September 18, 2004

Introduction

As two sisters brought up and married in St. Louis, we saw a huge need for *The St. Louis Wedding Book*. Newly engaged, we started our wedding planning at the bridal shows. They were a lot of fun but left us overwhelmed and unorganized. The Yellow Pages and the Internet left us just as confused as to where and how to start planning. We needed a quick and easy wedding guide to give us an overview of all of our wedding choices. We needed a comprehensive listing of our favorites with at-a-glance facts to answer all our questions. Finally, we needed a guide to help us plan the coolest wedding at the best cost possible. So here you have it! *The St. Louis Wedding Book* will not only save you time and money but also make your wedding planning easy and enjoyable.

We have worked hard to make sure the information contained in this book is as up-to-date as possible, but websites, phone numbers and prices are always subject to change. For each entry, we have provided a pricing guide to help you plan your budget, but keep in mind that final prices will depend on your specific choices.

In researching this book, we talked to numerous representatives and selected the best that St. Louis has to offer. We have included only those that made great impressions on us, but don't worry—

that doesn't mean all of your options have to be top-end. We located services in all price ranges, in all styles, so you can create the wedding that's best for *you!*

As you plan your wedding, remember what things are important to you. Don't get carried away with pleasing others. If you have a list of three areas that are most important to you and your soon-to-be spouse, it will be easier to prioritize where to spend your money.

In this book we cover all aspects of planning a wedding, beginning with choosing a site for the ceremony and finding an officiant. Then we take you through finding the right reception site, choosing a caterer, and selecting your music. We also cover photographers, videographers, and florists. Naturally, you will need a cake, and don't forget transportation! Finally, we offer listings for stationery companies, bride's and groom's attire, and finally, all the other details that make your day so special. So dive right in and get started! We're going to help you plan the wedding of your dreams.

Planning Timeline

12 – 18 months

- ☐ Choose the date of your big day.
- ☐ Reserve ceremony location.
- ☐ Interview and choose your wedding officiant.
- ☐ Interview and choose your reception location.
- ☐ Interview and choose your photographer and videographer.

9 – 12 months

- ☐ Interview and choose your caterer.
- ☐ Interview and choose your entertainment.
- ☐ Schedule bridal attire appointments.
  Visit at least three bridal stores.
- ☐ Mail the Save-the-Date cards.

6 – 9 months

- ☐ Order bridal gown.
- ☐ Decide on bridesmaids' dresses and order.
- ☐ Interview and choose transportation.
- ☐ Interview and choose your florist.
- ☐ Interview stationer and order your stationery.
- ☐ Rent and reserve tuxedos for groom and the wedding party.

3 – 6 months

- ☐ Interview bakeries and order cake or dessert.
- ☐ Follow up with ceremony location about your reservation.
- ☐ Meet with reception venue or caterer for a tasting of cuisine.
- ☐ Finalize the menu with your reception venue or caterer.
- ☐ Discuss the wedding service with your officiant.
- ☐ Confirm rental equipment for ceremony.
- ☐ Complete the guest list for headcount.
- ☐ Order flowers.
- ☐ Mail invitations.

2 months

- [ ] Update headcount and confirm the menu.
- [ ] Give your live band any requested songs that they might need to learn.
- [ ] Schedule the first dress fitting.

1 month

- [ ] Finalize and confirm all ceremony and reception plans.
- [ ] Finalize and confirm details with the photographer and videographer including a list of your must-have shots.
- [ ] Arrange transportation for out-of-town guests.
- [ ] Schedule your last dress fitting and a possible pickup.
- [ ] Finalize tuxedo alterations.
- [ ] Call any guests that haven't responded.
- [ ] Plan seating arrangements for reception.
- [ ] Make table, menu, and place cards if needed.

1 – 2 weeks

- [ ] Confirm with all vendors.
- [ ] Give final headcount to caterer.
- [ ] Provide a song list to your musicians or DJ detailing songs you want and don't want played. Include song requests.

1. Ceremonies and Officiants

The ceremony is the focal point of your wedding in which all eyes will be on the bride! The ceremony location and officiant account for about 3 percent of your budget and you'll have three basic choices for each. Your ceremony will either take place in a house of worship, at a non-traditional site, or at your reception location.

Most houses of worship such as churches, synagogues, or chapels provide their own officiant. If you're interested in using your own clergy in a house of worship you'll need to check to see if outside clergy are allowed. If choosing a more non-traditional site for your ceremony such as parks, the zoo, a butterfly house, or your reception location, you'll need to provide your own officiant.

There are three main places to find an officiant for your ceremony, including your home place of worship, a clergy service (listed in this book), or a friend who's been ordained. We've listed mostly nontraditional places of worship where outside clergy are allowed to officiate as well as other non-traditional ceremony locations. We've also provided a few clergy services.

the St. Louis Wedding Book

Timeline

12 – 18 months
- Reserve ceremony location.
- Interview and choose your wedding officiant.

3 – 6 months
- Follow up with ceremony location about your reservation.
- Discuss the wedding service with your officiant.
- Confirm rental equipment for ceremony.

1 month
- Finalize and confirm all ceremony plans.
- Finalize and confirm details with the officiant.

1 – 2 weeks
- Finalize confirmation with ceremony site and officiant.

👍 / Do's & / Don'ts 👎

- Remember to consider the season when choosing your location. If you select an outdoor setting, plan an alternate location in case of inclement weather.

- Think about planning your ceremony fairly close to your reception for the ease of your guests.

- Make sure there is space at the ceremony location to wait until the ceremony begins. You don't want to show everyone your dress before "show time."

- Ask the ceremony coordinator if there is ample time before and after the ceremony in case it runs over, to take pictures, and to talk with guests. (Some locations have multiple weddings throughout the day.)

💰 Money-Saving Tips

- Pick an outdoor location such as a park. Most likely you will just pay the price of the permit, and the natural beauty of the surroundings means you don't need to provide any additional decoration.

- Choose a chapel that is already simply decorated with plants and flowers. Use your own ribbons for the aisles.

- Purchase the ring pillow, unity candle, and guest book at a craft store and add your own decorations to them.

- Use a friend or family member that is an ordained ceremony officiant.

The Ceremony

If you belong to a parish or synagogue,
you may opt to have your wedding ceremony there.
However, if you are interested in a less traditional location,
consider one of these beautiful settings.

Questions to ask your Ceremony Location

- What is the facility fee?
- How much time is allowed for the service?
- How many people will the facility hold?
- Are any decorations included? Can I provide my own?
- Are there any restrictions on flowers or candles?
- Are there accessible restrooms available?
- What items are included and what should I provide (i.e., aisle runners, microphone, music)?
- Are there dressing rooms available for the bridal party?
- Are there any rules regarding photography inside the facility?
- Are there any music restrictions?

The Butterfly House

15193 Olive Boulevard | Chesterfield, Missouri 63017
636 530 0076
www.butterflyhouse.org
Capacity: up to 150 guests | Rental fee: $1,200

The Butterfly House, a division of the Missouri Botanical Garden, located in Faust Park is a wonderful place to hold an outside wedding. Within the Butterfly House grounds, there are three locations where a ceremony can take place: the Monsanto Pavilion, the Butterfly Garden Deck, or the Emerson Lakeside Terrace and Pavilion.

The Monsanto Pavilion is positioned on a hill with lavish gardens and a brook and is arranged with 20-foot white cloth from ceiling to floor. The Butterfly Garden Deck surrounds a pond, which creates a beautiful atmosphere. The Emerson Lakeside Terrace and Pavilion backs up to the lake, which has an enormous lighted fountain situated in the middle. A tent can be attached to the roofline of the pavilion for additional guests. Also, the pavilion and tent have ceiling fans and can be heated to accommodate weather conditions.

The wedding season spans from May 1 to mid-October, and they hold ceremonies on both Saturdays and Sundays at 11:00 a.m. and 2:00 p.m. During both July and August, the Butterfly House also includes Friday and Saturday evenings for weddings at either 6:30 or 7:30 p.m. The rental fee includes a rehearsal, use of the area for two hours, chairs for up to 150 guests, use of a sound system with microphones, guests' admission to the Butterfly Conservatory, free parking, and event supervision.

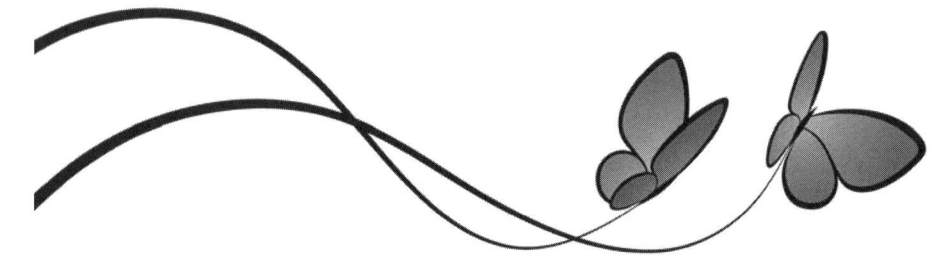

Carondelet Park

South Grand Boulevard and Loughborough Avenue
St. Louis, Missouri 63116
314 289 5344
www.stlouis.missouri.org
Capacity: up to 250 guests | Rental fee: $500

Carondelet Park is the third largest park in St. Louis and is a magnificent place for a wedding ceremony. The large lakes, green rolling hills, and fountains offer a charming setting. There are two locations to rent for ceremonies, the Boathouse and the Music Stand, both offering a perfect place to exchange vows.

The enormous Boathouse comes complete with a small pagoda on the edge of the lake. The Music Stand includes a patio and a small covered pavilion. Both the Boathouse and Music Stand have a roof, but the windows are open. Each offers electricity for live music or a complete sound system.

The rental fee for each location includes the space for up to four hours. Chairs, tables, or other equipment would have to be acquired from another source.

If you have some room in your budget,
try **idoweddingmaps.com** or
weddingmap.com to design your
own wedding map.

Church of the Open Word Garden Chapel

1040 Dautel Lane | St. Louis, Missouri 63146
314 872 7124
www.openwordchurch.org
Capacity: up to 150 guests
Rental fee: Weekdays $350 – $700; weekends $600 – $900

Church of the Open Word Garden Chapel is a wonderful place for a wedding ceremony. It has an elegant indoor setting that easily holds 125 guests and an outdoor setting that holds 150 guests. The chapel comes complete with abundant outdoor gardens, perfect for photos.

The rental fee includes the minister, wedding coordinator, hostess, setup, candelabras, recorded music, dressing room, and ample parking. A piano and organ are obtainable with a professional organist with prior notice and a fee. The chapel is available to the bridal party an hour before the ceremony for a total of two hours.

A short rehearsal on Wednesday evening prior to the ceremony is available at no extra charge, but a rehearsal Thursday or Friday evening is subject to an additional fee. The Church of the Open Word will welcome any officiant to lead weddings in the chapel, so if you have one in mind, feel free to use him or her.

Eliot Chapel

216 E. Argonne | Kirkwood, Missouri 63122
Mailing address: 100 S. Taylor Avenue | Kirkwood, Missouri 63122
314 821 0911
www.eliotchapel.org
Capacity: 235 guests | Rental fee: $825

Eliot Chapel is a charming stone non-denominational chapel located in beautiful Kirkwood. Emily attended a wedding here a couple of years ago and thought it was a perfect place to hold a ceremony, especially if you are not a member of a religious congregation. The sanctuary holds 235 guests. The fee includes the minister, wedding coordinator, rooms for the wedding party to dress, two flower pedestals, guest book stand, and the unity candle holder. When booking a ceremony, the chapel is reserved for three hours. There is a sound system available for recorded music, but there is an extra charge for a technician to operate it during the ceremony. Also available is a piano for your use, and silk floral decorations are available for rental.

Ethical Society of St. Louis

9001 Clayton Road | St. Louis, Missouri 63117
314 991 0955
www.ethicalstl.org
Capacity: up to 420 guests | Rental fee: $275 and up

Ethical Society of St. Louis is centrally located with abundant parking and has multiple areas within, perfect for any size ceremony. The auditorium holds 420 guests and offers a relaxed, personal setting for simple or elaborate weddings. It has a grand piano and a tracker organ, which is one of only a few around the area. The foyer is an ideal spot for a very small wedding of under 50 guests. It is designed with three walls of stained glass, so no need for decorations—the room just sparkles. The officiants within the Ethical Culture offer non-denominational ceremonies focused on the couple and the commitment they are making to each other. You may also bring your own clergy to officiate your ceremony.

The Jewel Box

In Forest Park | St. Louis, Missouri 63110
314 531 0080
http://stlouis.missouri.org
Capacity: up to 250 guests | Rental fee: $900

The Jewel Box, located in Forest Park, is an extremely stunning and admired spot to have your wedding ceremony all year round. Reservations can be taken two years in advance, and it books up quickly. If there is an opening and you book your ceremony less than a year in advance, there is a discount rate of $500. Weddings are performed in one-and-a-half-hour increments, and all pictures, ceremony, and so forth, must happen in the contracted time. The rental fee includes 250 chairs and the space. Sound systems or a microphone must be rented from another source.

Kiener Plaza & Morton D. May Amphitheater

500–700 Pine Street | St. Louis, Missouri 63101
314 289 5300
http://stlouis.missouri.org
Capacity: up to 3,000 guests | Rental fee: $300

For all you true St. Louisans, this is a perfect place for an outdoor wedding. The famous Arch and Old Courthouse create a fabulous backdrop. In the center of Kiener Plaza is a huge pool and fountain with a statue in the center. The rental fee is for a four-hour time slot and includes the space for 3,000 guests. Chairs or other required equipment would need to be rented from another supplier. Kiener Plaza doesn't have bathrooms, so you will want to think of alternative arrangements for your guests. If you are looking for an ideal spot for an outdoor wedding and love the feel of downtown St. Louis, check it out!

World's Fair Pavilion

In Forest Park | St. Louis, Missouri 63110
314 289 5344
http://stlouis.missouri.org
Capacity: up to 500 guests | Rental fee: $700 or $900

World's Fair Pavilion is a famous open-air shelter located in Forest Park. It's one of the park's most beautiful and admired attractions and was originally built in 1909 with proceeds from the 1904 World's Fair. It was completely renovated in 1998 and creates the setting of your dreams. The space has room for 500 guests under the shelter, or you may use the surrounding park grounds for a bigger crowd. If you have your heart set on an evening wedding, don't sweat because the dimmer switches underneath the pavilion create the perfect atmosphere for any event. The rental fee includes the area. Chairs or equipment have to be obtained from another source. Accessible restrooms are available. World's Fair Pavilion can also hold receptions. (See Chapter 2, "Receptions.")

Go green and visit **weddingmapper.com** to set up a free online map, connecting all the landmarks of your wedding, from ceremony to reception site to hotels. You can even suggest restaurants and attractions for your out-of-town guests. Include a link to your map in your invitations and guests can plan their trip and customize their driving directions.

Visit **weddingmapper.com** or **googlemaps.com** to create a free printable map to include with your invitations.

Officiants

Choosing your wedding officiant is an important decision because it sets the tone of the whole ceremony. You will want to find the right person who is willing to perform the style of ceremony you want. Look for someone who is flexible and comfortable performing the type of ceremony you desire. Also, make sure the officiant is approved in the state you are getting married in to legally marry you.

Questions to ask your Officiant

- How long have you been performing weddings?
- Do you have sample ceremony readings to choose from?
- Can we specify details such as readings and vows?
- Are you open to personalized readings and music?
- Are you available for a rehearsal?

All Couples Married

314 781 0444
www.allcouplesmarried.com
Fee: Call for pricing

All Couples Married is comprised of multiple ministers who are non-denominational officiants performing wedding ceremonies customized to your liking. They perform ceremonies at parks, reception venues, restaurants, and home settings. Whether you are looking for something simple or detailed, they can write vows that suit your desires. They tend to book up fast, so reserve early. Pricing depends on times, dates, and availability.

Assisi Weddings

314 651 9663
www.assisiweddings.com
Fee: Call for pricing

Bishop Frederick J. Sansone has been performing weddings for more than 25 years. He specializes in ceremonies of all faiths, religious or nonreligious. Bishop Sansone will travel to the location of your choice, serving Missouri and Illinois. Visit his website or give him a call to set up an appointment.

Notes

Notes

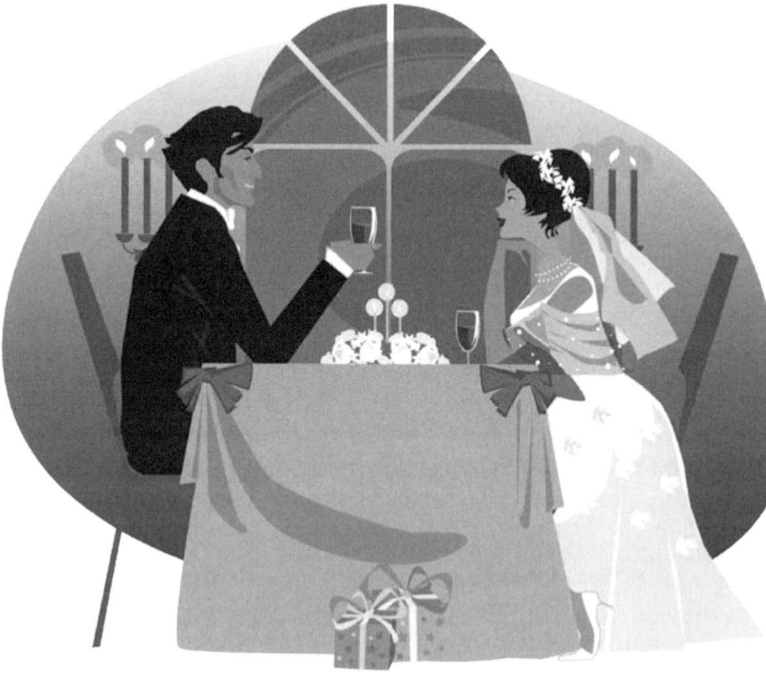

2. Receptions

Your reception location is one of the biggest decisions you'll make for your wedding because it accounts for around 50 percent of your budget and you'll spend between two and eight hours there. Keep in mind that most venues we spoke with are willing to work with your budget, so be honest about how much money you have to work with and find out what they can do for you. There are many aspects to consider when choosing your reception site.

First you'll need a very rough estimate of how many guests you expect will attend (usually expect about 80 percent of the guests invited to actually attend) so you can choose a venue to fit the number of guests attending.

Next, choose which type of location you want. Consider having the venue reflect your occupations, hobbies, hometown, home state, or nationality. Having the reception where you met would be a fun idea, too. If the bride or groom is a wine connoisseur, you might choose Mount Pleasant Winery; artists, the Randall Gallery, Mad Art, or City Museum; lawyers or history buffs, the History Museum; naturalists, the Zoo, Butterfly House, Science Center, or Botanical Gardens; musicians, Powell Symphony Hall. Mad Art would also be fun for police officers as it was originally a 1930s police station and still houses some jail cells. If you are of Italian descent, consider Favazza's on the Hill. If you met somewhere in St. Louis, have your reception (or rehearsal dinner) at that location.

For example, maybe you met, had your first date, or celebrated your first dating anniversary at The Tap Room, Sunset 44, Morgan Street, or the Melting Pot. Any of those places would be a wonderful setting for your reception.

Another aspect to think about is the season, because you can't very easily do outdoors in St. Louis during December through February. Also, you might want to consider your choice of entertainment—some reception locations have restrictions on the type of music you can have. In addition, some locations may drown out or be too confined for the type of music you have in mind. Consider whether or not you would like on-site catering or if you want to provide your own caterer. Finally, think about whether you'll have many out-of-town guests and the distance of the ceremony from the reception. Coordinating your ceremony and reception site with their hotel(s) will make the day more enjoyable for your guests.

Below we have included a cost key to describe the average price on a Saturday night for food and open bar per person. Besides the food and bar cost, there may be many other additional expenses such as hors d'oeuvres, cake, decorations, and other amenities. Prices are always subject to change. The cost key is for general budgeting purposes only.

Money-Saving Tips

- Choose a park for your reception location. Many parks have beautiful pavilions that have a fairly reasonable rental fee.
- Have your reception in the late morning or early afternoon, which will cut costs on the food, alcohol, and rental fees.
- Friday nights tend to be more affordable than Saturdays.
- Have hors d'oeuvres or a buffet rather than a sit-down meal.
- To save on bar cost, skip the open bar or limit the choices for drinks.
- Fill clear vases with fruit for table centerpieces.

Cost Key

$	under $30
$$	$30 - $50
$$$	$51 - $70
$$$$	$71 - $90
$$$$$	over $90

Anheuser-Busch Center

1 Soccer Park Road | Fenton, Missouri 63026 | 636 343 5347
www.absoccerpark.com
Capacity: Up to 250 guests | Rental fee: $200 to $1,400
Cost: $$

Imagine having your wedding reception at a facility owned by a corporation that is known across the world and based right here in the St. Louis area. Well, Anheuser-Busch has the perfect place, located in Fenton, where we grew up. There are various rooms to choose from depending on the size of your party. Some of the room amenities include an enormous marble fireplace, cherry wood walls, granite panels, full bar, and a veranda enclosed in glass, looking out on 35 acres of beautiful grounds. An extensive kitchen and executive chef is on hand, which is helpful, and the staff can even create an exciting themed buffet such as Italian, German, or New Orleans style.

Busch Stadium

250 Stadium Plaza | St. Louis , Missouri 63102 | 314 345 9000
www.cardinals.mlb.com
Capacity: Up to 45,000 guests | Rental fee: $400 to $10,000
Cost: $$$

Are you a Cardinals fan? Busch Stadium has become one of St. Louis' admired spots for a wedding reception. They offer 15 different spaces for your venue that can accommodate any type of celebration whether it is large or small, formal or informal, indoors or out. Sportservice is their exclusive caterer, offering a substantial amount of selection on their menu. Some of the unique amenities that can be added to your reception package include: Fredbird appearance, on-field photos, scoreboard messages and much more. Keep in mind that your event cannot be held on a game day.

Questions to Ask Your Reception Location

- Is our preferred date available?
- How many other receptions are taking place the same day as ours?
- What is the rental fee and what's included?
- Do you offer any packages (food, drinks, flowers, cake, entertainment, etc.)?
- Is there a cake-cutting fee?
- Can the food be sampled?
- What decorations do you include or are there options for providing our own?
- How many hours will we have for the reception?
- Is there accessible parking and is parking free?
- Are there any restrictions regarding using this facility (rules regarding smoking, candles, etc.)?
- Will staff be available the day of the event?
- Does the facility provide guest accommodation discounts and are there convenient locations nearby?

The Butterfly House

15193 Olive Boulevard
Chesterfield, Missouri 63017
636 733 2339
www.butterflyhouse.org
Capacity: Up to 200 guests
Rental fee: $2,100 to $2,900
Cost: Depends on caterer

The Butterfly House, located in Faust Park, is a great place for an outdoor wedding reception. All receptions take place on the Emerson Terrace and Pavilion, which is positioned on the lake, complete with an enormous lighted fountain center and lined with lighted trees. How romantic! The reception package includes use of the pavilion from 5:30 p.m. to 11:00 p.m., rental of the dining tables and chairs, bride's room, admission to the butterfly conservatory for all guests, free parking, and supervision for the whole event. The Butterfly House has arrangements with three spectacular caterers in the area: Hendri's Catering, Russo's Catering, and Patty Long Catering, each offering everything from hors d'oeuvres to a complete buffet or seated dinner. (See Chapter 1, "Ceremonies and Officiants," and Chapter 3, "Catering," for more information.)

Chase Park Plaza

212-232 N. Kingshighway Boulevard | St. Louis, MO 63108
314 633 3050
www.chaseparkplaza.com
Capacity: 75 to 2,500 guests | Rental fee and cost: $$$-$$$$

Chase Park Plaza has dazzling reception rooms but also a movie theater, salon and spa, tanning spa, barbershop, heated outdoor pool, fitness center, car rental, very modish bars, and contemporary restaurants—all on-site! Plus, it's located within walking distance of the Central West End's trendy restaurants and shopping. The Chase Park Plaza offers many different rooms for receptions. The Starlight Roof is the most popular choice with its wall of floor-to-ceiling windows overlooking Forest Park. Receptions include catering, floral and table arrangements, valet parking, accommodations for guests, plus much more. You can't go wrong with all the on-site amenities available.

The City Museum

701 N. 15th Street | St. Louis, MO 63103
314 231 2489 ext. 117
www.citymuseum.org
Capacity: Up to 400 guests
Rental fee: $500 to $3,500 | Cost: Depends on caterer

The City Museum is a three-story facility adorned with recycled materials constructed into amazing mosaics, sculptures, and interactive art. There isn't a square inch of wall, ceiling, or floor that isn't enveloped in art. The City Museum has numerous rental solutions with the ability to accommodate any number of guests up to 400. Five key areas are available for rental: The City Museum Package (Architecture Hall, First Floor, and Mezzanine), First Floor Mezzanine, Architecture Hall, Cabin Inn and Patio, and the Vault Room. Each area is unique and elegant in every way imaginable. The City Museum also has nine different caterers to choose from.

The Falls Reception and Conference Center

300 Admiral Weinel Boulevard | Columbia, Illinois 62236
618 281 3255
www.seethefalls.com
Capacity: Up to 600 guests | Rental fee: None | Cost: $$

All wedding packages include champagne toast, cake, DJ, linens and china, event coordinator, and discounted invitations. For your convenience, two limos are available for rental; you can have your tuxedo rental return at The Falls, and a bridal suite with hors d'oeuvres is available. You can hold your ceremony for up to 200 guests in front of the waterfalls. Additionally, they hold food tastings once a month. Although they have three separate banquet rooms that can be opened up to accommodate larger parties, they never hold more than two weddings per night. The location is easy to find (even if you're terrible with directions like us) and has ample, well-lit parking. In addition to the plethora of wedding planning conveniences, they have waterfalls indoors and outdoors for great photo opportunities.

Favazza's Rose of the Hill

2300 Edwards | St. Louis, Missouri 63110 | 314 772 6003
www.roseofthehill.com
Capacity: 50 to 500 guests | Rental fee: $750 | Cost: $$

For a little bit of Italy in St. Louis' historic "Hill" neighborhood, try this traditional favorite. The Old World–style ambiance includes marble columns, 35-foot dark wood bar, dark wood chairs, and classic artwork. This romantic space for bride, groom, and guests offers amenities such as cake by Missouri Bakery, centerpieces with candles, decorated head table, gift and cake table, and a champagne toast for the head table. Top this off with a renowned Italian meal for a memorable wedding celebration.

Hendri's

4501 Ridgewood Avenue | St. Louis, Missouri 63116 | 314 752 4084
www.hendris.com
Capacity: 50 to 300 guests | Rental fee: None | Cost: $$

Hendri's is definitely a place that we would highly recommend. We both think it's a great location with great service, and it's reasonably priced. Before visiting Hendri's, we had never heard of this venue, but as soon as the doors were opened, our mouths dropped. The room is absolutely fabulous. All you can focus on is the black-and-white checkered floors, the dark cherry wood walls, and the enormous cherry wood bar. Let us not forget the huge fireplace that makes the room sparkle. After visiting ourselves, we recommended it to our friends, Tommy and Lyzzi, and they had their reception here and were more than pleased. They said the cuisine was delicious and the staff was extremely accommodating. Hendri's is a single-room facility, so the place is yours for the night. Also, Hendri's provides catering, so the menu is extensive and they can even create themes and ethnic creations.

Holiday Inn Southwest

10709 Watson Road | St. Louis, Missouri 63127 | 314 821 6600
www.hiviking.com
Capacity: Up to 500 guests | Rental fee: None | Cost: $$

Allison had her reception here in August 2001 and recommends it as an affordable, all-inclusive choice for anyone with a lot of out-of-town guests. Her husband's family is from out of state as is her extended family, so she knew she wanted to have her reception at a hotel. She was looking for a reasonably priced establishment located close to interstates, her church, shops, and restaurants. Being an easygoing couple, Allison and Brian found this location suited them best because everything was included: cake, flowers, decorations, plus a block of discounted rooms, pool, and nightclub on-site for guests. The entire evening went as smoothly as the planning of the event.

Kemoll's / Top of the Met

1 Metropolitan Square | St. Louis, MO 63102 | 314 783 0667
www.kemolls.com
Capacity: Up to 265 guests | Rental fee: $500 for the Top of the Met
Cost: $$$$

Kemoll's is an award-winning restaurant located inside the famous Metropolitan Square within the heart of downtown St. Louis. Kemoll's has been entertaining since 1927 by serving delectable cuisine and offering remarkable service. The restaurant has an enormous banquet facility, called Top of the Met, on the glorious 42nd floor holding 265 guests. The Top of the Met has massive windows overlooking Saint Louis' own riverfront as well as striking images of the famous skyline. There are also five elegant dining rooms just below the Top of the Met on the 40th floor that hold from 10 to 250 people. Packages include free garage parking, white linens, and centerpieces.

Le Chateau

10405 Clayton Road | St. Louis, MO 63131 | 314 991 6700
www.cesandjudys.com
Capacity: Up to 300 guests | Rental fee: None
Cost: $$$

Located in Frontenac, Le Chateau, with its European influence, gives visitors the feeling that they just stepped into a tiny village in France. Le Chateau has two elegant rooms to choose from, or you can combine them to accommodate a larger group of guests. The Round Room has high ceilings, a fireplace, and corresponding staircases leading up to a lovely balcony. The large banquet room is just as charming with sparkling chandeliers and a wooden dance floor. One bonus about having your reception here is that everything from china to a mouth-watering cake is included in your event package, so no need to look elsewhere for a caterer—there is one on-site.

Lemp Mansion

3322 DeMenil Place | St. Louis, Missouri 63118 | 314 664 8024
www.lempmansion.com
Capacity: Up to 300 guests | Rental fee: $700 or $1200
Cost: $$

Lemp Mansion is one of the many historic landmarks of St. Louis owned by Patty Pointer and Mary Wolff. We were impressed with the facility and especially Patty, with whom we spoke when we visited. Throughout our research, we have learned to love family-owned businesses, and Lemp is no exception. It has two great areas to have your wedding reception, the dazzling Gazebo with outdoor patio and the Grand Hall. The outdoor patio can be tented, which is so elegant. The Grand Hall is magnificent. You ride in an old-style elevator that reveals a gorgeous room with maple flooring and an enormous bar. It also has a huge rooftop patio with rod iron furniture covered in twinkle lights. Packages include a four-hour bar, McArthur's cake, a champagne toast, centerpieces, tables, chairs, linens, china, silverware, glassware, and more.

Mad Art Gallery

2727 S. 12th Street | St. Louis, Missouri 63118 | 314 771 3202
www.madart.com
Capacity: Up to 500 guests | Rental fee: $2,000
Cost: Depends on caterer

Mad Art, located in historic Soulard, is a 1930s police station that was renovated into a modern art gallery and an exceptional setting for an Art Deco wedding reception. Marble floors, classy artwork, and an outstanding courtyard with an outdoor fireplace that can be viewed from indoors through the glass garage door are just a few amenities that Mad Art offers. Preferred caterers are offered but Mad Art provides their own bar service. Wedding packages include tables and chairs. If you are looking for something unique rather than traditional, Mad Art is the place you have been searching for.

The Magic House

516 S. Kirkwood Road | St. Louis, Missouri 63122 | 314 822 8900 ext. 20
www.magichouse.org
Capacity: Up to 1,000 guests | Rental fee: $500 to $2,500
Cost: Depends on the caterer

For a unique setting try the famous Magic House. Because they usually hold one wedding per weekend during the peak season, they aren't lacking in experience as you might expect from such a distinctive venue. Couples are able to rent the entire Magic House for larger receptions or rent individual rooms for a smaller event. This venue also offers outdoor areas that include fabulous landscaped gardens, an open-air Victorian Pavilion, waterfalls, a walk-around porch, and more. Your guests are free to explore the Magic House, which makes for interesting photo opportunities. Other notable aspects include the opportunity for a group photo on the Magic House porch, their willingness to work with your budget, and the versatility of the house.

Mahler Ballroom

4915 Washington Avenue | St. Louis, Missouri 63108
314 361 4411
www.mahlerballroom.com
Capacity: Up to 200 guests | Cost: Depends on caterer

The Mahler Ballroom was once a legendary ballroom, making it one of Saint Louis' precious gems today. Located in the heart of the Central West End, today it is a Victorian-style banquet facility. Its elaborate balcony can seat up to 250 of your guests and offers a great view of the enormous historic dance floor. Outside caterers are welcome, and Mahler provides full bar service.

Marriott West

660 Maryville Centre Drive | St. Louis, Missouri 63141 | 314 878 2747
www.marriottstlouisweddings.com
(website has Resources for the Bride section that includes a Planning Kit & Wedding Calculator)
Capacity: Up to 1,000 guests | Rental fee: None
Cost: $$$-$$$$

Marriott West is an impressive spot to hold your reception if you're expecting out-of-town guests. It's near the airport, Westport Plaza, and Chesterfield. It's also very accessible to downtown and other St. Louis attractions. They can accommodate anything from an elaborate gala to an intimate celebration. Marriott West prides itself on customer service, so couples work with a certified wedding planner from day one to the day of the event. They offer everything from a champagne brunch to a formal sit-down dinner. Some of the items that are included in the reception package are passed hors d'oeuvres, champagne toast, complimentary overnight stay for the couple, specialty linens, centerpieces, and much more.

Melting Pot

294 Lamp and Lantern Village | Town and Country, Missouri 63017
636 207 6358
www.meltingpot.com
Capacity: Up to 50 guests
Rental fee: none but there is a minimum cost of $1,500 during the week and $2,000 during the weekend | Cost: $$$

The Melting Pot, with locations in Town and Country and University City, is an impressive spot to hold a wedding shower, rehearsal dinner, or intimate wedding reception. This fondue restaurant offers up to a four-course meal that you prepare at your table including cheese fondue, salad, main entrée, and/or chocolate fondue. Main entrée selections include beef, chicken, duck, lobster, shrimp, scallops, and fish fillet. The feature we like about the Melting Pot is the intimate dining experience. From the first course to the last, the meal usually takes about two and a half hours, which gives you special time to visit with close friends and family. If you are looking for an exclusive, personal setting, check out the Melting Pot.

Missouri Botanical Garden

4344 Shaw Boulevard | St. Louis, Missouri 63110
314 577 0200
http://www.mobot.org
Capacity: Up to 380 guests | Rental fee: $250 to $2,000
Cost: $$-$$$$

Naturalists take note! Rent the entire gorgeous Garden or choose one of three indoor facilities: the Spink Pavilion, Monsanto Hall, or the Shoenberg Auditorium. Events at The Garden are planned by Catering St. Louis. Their menu is outstanding whether you're planning a hors d'oeuvres cocktail party, a seated dinner, or anything in between.

Missouri Historical Society and Museum

5700 Lindell Avenue (at DeBaliviere) in Forest Park
St. Louis, Missouri 63112
314 454 3154 or 314 454 3151
www.mohistory.org
Capacity: Up to 300 guests | Rental fee: $2000
Cost: $$$$-$$$$$

A must for history buffs! The History Museum's new Emerson Center just opened in 2000. It has two huge facilities for events: MacDermott Grand Hall and the Meriweather Restaurant. The Grand Hall has a modern feel with high ceilings and glass walls. The River Mosaic runs from wall to wall, and the Spirit of St. Louis replica hangs in the center. The Meriweather Restaurant, another bright choice, is located on the top floor of the Emerson Center. The glass wall overlooking Forest Park gives a beautiful view for your guests. Impress your guests: this location was featured on Food Network's "Best of Museum Restaurants."

Morgan Street Brewery

721 N. Second Street | St. Louis, Missouri 63102
314 231 9970
www.morganstreetbrewery.com
Capacity: Up to 200 guests | Rental fee: $50 to $500
Cost: $$

For an intimate reception on St. Louis' famous riverfront with plenty of nightlife nearby, try Morgan Street Brewery. Cross cobblestone into this pub-style brewery with brick walls and wrought-iron gates surrounding the patio. Whether you're into a casual reception or a more elegant setting, the brewery has an array of rooms. To complement the room selection, this venue has a menu just as diverse.

Mount Pleasant Winery

5634 High Street | Augusta, Missouri 63332
636 482 WINE ext. 243   636 482 WINE   ext 227
www.mountpleasant.com
Capacity: Up to 750 guests | Rental fee: $500 to $2,400
Cost: Depends on caterer

Located in Augusta, not far from St. Charles, Washington, and St. Louis, Mount Pleasant Winery is gorgeous and not as expensive as you might expect. Although smaller areas are available, the main reception areas are the Terrace Ballroom and Mount Pleasant Arbor. They offer a handful of caterers to choose from, and Mount Pleasant is open all year round.

Ninth Street Abbey (and Patty Long Catering)

1808 S. Ninth Street | St. Louis, Missouri 63104 | 314 621 9598
www.pattylongcatering.com
Capacity: Up to 250 guests | Rental fee: $1,000 | Cost: $$$

Ninth Street Abbey in historic Soulard is catered by Patty Long Catering, who has more than 20 years' catering experience. Besides featuring the caterer named numerous times as the best in St. Louis (see Chapter 3, "Catering," for more information on Patty Long Catering), your reception will be held in a timeless restored church with cathedral ceilings, a large wood bar, original stained-glass windows, and adjoining outdoor patio. The Abbey seats 250 guests inside, and the rooftop deck seats up to 50 for a more intimate setting. The rooftop deck is a bright sunroom with windows opening up the brick walls and overlooking the garden below. A few amenities that the Abbey offers are candelabras, eight-foot white pillars, and a Grand Piano.

Old Hickory Golf Club

1 Dye Club Drive | St. Peters, Missouri 63304 | 636 477 8960
www.oldhickorygc.com
Capacity: Up to 800 guests | Rental fee: None
Cost: $$-$$$

Allison was sold on this facility as soon as she pulled through the gates. Past the gates, she drove down a winding road through huge trees and a beautifully manicured golf course. The course is home to three lakes, and the new clubhouse facility's wall of windows overlooks one of the sparkling lakes. Old Hickory accommodates up to three weddings a weekend, every weekend from May through October. Besides complimentary linens, china and glassware, mirrored tiles, and votive candles, some unique additional services available are the chocolate fountains, champagne fountains, and ice sculptures. When the empty rooms already look as gorgeous as these, you know you have a winner.

Orlando Gardens

4300 Hoffmeister Avenue
St. Louis, Missouri 63125
314 638 6660

8352 Watson Road
St. Louis, Missouri 63119
314 638 6660

2050 Dorsett Village Plaza
Maryland Heights, Missouri 63043
314 453 9000

Lodge at Grant's Trail by Orlando's
4398 Hoffmeister Avenue,
St. Louis, MO, 63125
314 638 3340

www.orlandogardens.com
Capacity: Up to 850
Rental fee: None
Cost: $

If you are looking for an affordable banquet center with a lot of experience and top-notch customer service, check out Orlando Gardens. This family-owned business has more than 40 years of experience and accommodates 1,000 weddings a year at four banquet centers. We have been to weddings at the South County and Maryland Heights locations and had a great time at both. For ease of planning, Orlando will provide everything except your entertainment. Guests love the food and great service from a friendly, dedicated staff. Other available options to make your reception unique include chocolate fountains, a dessert station, and a coffee bar.

Timeline

12 – 18 months
- Choose the date of your big day.
- Interview and choose your reception location.

3 – 6 months
- Meet with reception venue or caterer for a tasting of cuisine.
- Finalize the menu with your reception venue.
- Complete the guest list for a headcount.

2 months
- Update headcount and confirm menu.

1 month
- Finalize and confirm all reception plans.
- Call any guests that haven't responded.
- Plan seating arrangements for reception.
- Make table, menu, and place cards if needed.

1 – 2 weeks
- Final confirmation with reception venue.
- Give final headcount.

Powell Symphony Hall

718 N. Grand Boulevard | St. Louis, Missouri 63103
314 286 4460
www.slso.org
Capacity: Up to 400 guests | Rental fee: $3,000
Cost: Depends on caterer

Have a classic, sophisticated wedding in mind? Picture yourself on your wedding day among the crystal chandeliers, scarlet curtains and carpet, and ivory and gold columns stretching to the towering ceilings that make Powell Symphony Hall so beautiful.

Originally built in 1925 as the Saint Louis Theatre, Powell Symphony Hall now features four breath-taking areas: the Grand Foyer, the Whitaker Room, the Met Bar, and the Auditorium. The Grand Foyer holds 140 to 400 guests and has complete bar service; the Whitaker Room accommodates 40 to 80 guests and also includes full bar service. From the old Metropolitan Opera House in New York, the Met Bar has a capacity of 40 to 100 guests. For a much larger reception, the auditorium holds up to 2,700 guests, including 15 tier boxes.

Facility rental fees are $2,000 for the ceremony and $3,000 for the reception and include security, cleaning, and house staff. They offer a full-service bar for $20 per person plus $75 per bartender with one bartender per 50 guests.

Catering, including table and chair rentals, is an additional cost, but you have the option of using their on-site caterers or bringing in your own.

Planning a honeymoon but don't have enough money left in the budget? Check out **www.honeymoonwishes.com** for a free honeymoon wedding registry.
Now your wedding guests can help pay for a trip to paradise.

Randall Gallery

999 N. 13th Street | St. Louis, Missouri 63106
314 231 4808
www.randallgallery.com
Capacity: Up to 650 guests | Rental fee: $495 to $1,495
Cost: $$$-$$$$$

Randall Gallery is a restored Civil War-era building in downtown St. Louis where the walls are climbing with modern art and large windows showcasing the city's bright lights. The hardwood floors, tall ceilings with track lighting, and 30-foot garden atrium with a beautiful fountain set the stage for a romantic atmosphere. The gallery is not active and is exclusively open for special events, so they can easily accommodate your every need. When holding your reception here, you have the entire facility to yourselves, which promises total concentration from the staff to make your celebration flawless. Another plus is a full kitchen on-site, so no need to find a caterer. Wedding packages include tables, chairs, linens, china and silverware, glassware, cutting and serving of the cake, silk ficus trees, and depending on your choice of wedding package, gallery centerpieces and stair decorations.

St. Louis Science Center

5050 Oakland Avenue | St. Louis, Missouri 63110
314 289 4471
www.slsc.org
Capacity: Up to 300 guests | Rental fee: $3,200
Cost: Depends on caterer

Looking for a wedding under the stars without the worry of inclement weather? The James S. McDonnell Planetarium is a beautiful setting for your reception with room for up to 300 guests under the star-filled ceiling. Or opt for a dinner for up to 100 friends and family on the bridge that crosses highway 40. Wedding packages include preferred catering, a four-hour event, tables and chairs, china service, free parking, and much more.

the St. Louis Wedding Book

St. Louis Zoo

1 Government Drive | St. Louis, Missouri 63110 | 314 646 4855
www.stlzoo.org
Capacity: Up to 1000 guests | Rental fee: Call for pricing
Cost: $$$

With four great facilities including the Living World, Event Tent, River Camp, and Lakeside Café, the St. Louis Zoo can hold almost any type of wedding you wish. The Living World is the largest facility and will hold up to 1,000 guests; it features beautiful wood floors and a 65-foot rotunda. The River Camp has three rooms that are available individually or combined to accommodate 200 guests. These rooms feature a private patio and a window into the Missouri River aquarium. Our personal favorite is the Event Tent, which can hold up to 800 guests—a huge white tent nestled just off of the River's Edge within gorgeous foliage near the hippos, hyenas, and rhinos. With plenty of room for a dance floor and tables beautifully displayed, you would never even know you were at the Zoo (minus a hyena or two cackling in the background). Our second favorite location is the Lakeside Café, lit with wall-mounted street lanterns. This option is located close to the Zoo's south entrance and will hold up to 300 guests indoors and up to 800 with the patio. The Zoo has its own full-service catering company that offers not only delicious food but also décor and entertainment.

> Our favorite free websites for designing your personalized wedding website are **momentville.com**, **projectwedding.com** and **weddingwire.com** or, as always, check out the popular sites such as **theknot.com**, **mywedding.com**, **ewedding.com** and **weddingchannel.com**.

Receptions

Schlafly Tap Room

2100 Locust Street | St. Louis, Missouri 63103 | 314 241 BEER
www.schlafly.com
Capacity: Up to 250 guests | Rental fee: $200 or $500
Cost: $-$$$

A great downtown location for intimate receptions, the Tap Room offers two rooms to choose from: The Club Room or The Eliot Room. With St. Louis' history of beer making, this famous microbrewery is the right setting for your reception. The Club Room includes a stage that is perfect for a DJ or live band and a personal outdoor balcony that faces the biergarten. The Eliot Room is smaller with large windows that open to historic downtown. It also has space for a DJ or live band and is located next to a large billiards room with pool tables and dart boards for your guests. Rental fee includes tables, chairs, table linens, china and silverware, votives for the table decoration, and a well-lit parking lot. It has a variety of menu options to choose from including appetizer packages, deluxe dinner packages, and everything in between.

Spazio's

12031 Lackland Road | St. Louis, Missouri 63146 | 314 576 0400
www.russosgourmet.com
Capacity: Up to 250 guests | Rental fee: None | Cost: $$-$$$

Spazio's, owned by Russo's Gourmet catering, has been in business since 1965 and is located in famous Westport Plaza. Close to restaurants, major highways, the airport, hotels, shops, dance clubs, and plenty of bars, it's a convenient place to hold any reception! Spazio's has three banquet rooms to choose from, the Ballroom, the Garden Room, and the Bistro. The rooms offer modern and classy décor and, depending on the room, outdoor patio and bilevel seating. We visited with Mark Russo, co-owner, who was very friendly and easy to work with. Wedding packages include a custom event planner, a four-hour open bar service, appetizer service, food service, wedding cake, linens, china, silverware, glassware, and decorations.

The Studio Inn at St. Albans

454 Studio Road | St. Albans, Missouri 63073 | 636 458 5356
www.studioinnstalbans.com
Capacity: Up to 240 guests | Rental fee: $250 to $3,900
Cost: $$$-$$$$$

Located 15 miles west of Chesterfield in the St. Albans Golf Course Community is The Studio Inn at St. Albans. The Studio Inn is really more of a stone castle nestled within trees on a hilltop overlooking a gorgeous valley. Originally built in 1923, it can accommodate you and 11 others on your wedding night if you so desire. It is newly renovated and will hold up to 120 guests seated inside the great room with a wall of windows overlooking the valley. Although both choices would be spectacular, the more common option chosen is the outdoor tent, which holds up to 225 guests. The outdoor ceremony site accommodates up to 120 seated. Receptions are catered exclusively by one of the restaurants in the area, The Gardens at Malmaison.

Sunset 44 Bistro and Banquet Center

118 W. Adams Avenue | Kirkwood, Missouri 63122 | 314 965 6644
www.sunset44.com
Capacity: Up to 260 guests
Rental fee: Only for parties of less than 20
Cost: $$$

Sunset 44 is owned by Bob Menendez, one of the most professional, experienced restaurant owners in the St. Louis area, who has been in the restaurant business for more than 40 years. Sunset 44 is one of our personal favorites because of the friendly, experienced staff, gourmet food, and classy décor. (Allison is friends with Bob's daughter Amy, so she might be a little biased.) Allison had one of her wedding showers here and has been here for a couple of baby showers as well. Couples love—and we would have to agree—the food prepared by three gourmet chefs and the customized menu options. The restaurant itself is great for large parties, and they have now opened a new banquet center with a gorgeous walnut dance floor. They offer media capabilities that include wireless Internet throughout, A/V systems, wireless microphones, plasma screens, surround sound, and LCD projectors. Other great features include an outdoor patio, more than 20 gourmet dinner entrees, plus customized menu options and wine bar with more than 200 wines to choose from.

Two Hearts Banquet and Conference Center

4532 S. Lindbergh Boulevard | Sunset Hills, Missouri 63127
314 843 8858
www.heartbanquets.com
Capacity: Up to 650 guests | Rental fee: None
Cost: $

If you are from the South County area, as we are, you know of Two Hearts. It's a white stone contemporary building at the corner of Lindbergh and Gravois that used to be Mark Twain Theatre. It reopened 20 years ago as Two Hearts and is the sister facility to the Heart of St. Charles. We love the large built-in wood bar and dance floor (it beats those flimsy portables that a lot of facilities offer); couples and their guests love the great food and organization. Packages include an event coordinator, linens, china, silverware, glassware, four-hour bar, a McArthur's cake cut and served, champagne toast for head table, and much more. If you opt for a buffet, they can serve a party of 400 within about 15 minutes so you don't have to worry about your guests sitting around waiting.

the St. Louis Wedding Book

Windows Off Washington

701 N. 15th Street, 10th Floor | St. Louis, Missouri 63103 | 314 241 5555
www.wowbanquets.com
Capacity: Up to 1000 guests | Rental fee: $850.00 to $1,250.00
Cost: $$$-$$$$$

Emily had her reception here in September 2004 and would highly recommend it to anyone interested in a modern, classy venue with a central downtown location. The panoramic view of the city's bright lights alone was enough to sell her. Not to mention the delectable entrees, accommodating staff, and contemporary atmosphere. Everything from the champagne greeting at the door to the chocolate mint departure made Emily and Paulo's wedding night flawless. Windows Off Washington even has a shuttle service to take guests to the free adjacent parking lot or downtown hotels afterward. They have winter and Friday night specials. Also check out their other venue, Windows On Washington.

Wildflower Loft

4 S. Euclid | St. Louis, Missouri 63108 | 314 361 8282
www.wildflowerloft.com
Capacity: Up to 200 guests | Rental fee: None
Cost: $$

Located in the heart of chic Central West End is Wildflower Loft Restaurant and Catering. Open since 2001, this venue offers some unique menu entrees including Cornish hens, stuffed pheasant, international stations (Italian, Mexican, Asian, and Cajun), and several vegetarian selections. They'll hold ceremonies for up to 150 guests. The receptions are held in a separate room upstairs from the restaurant, which has its own entrance. Brides love the charm of the restaurant and details covered by the staff. They will handle all details of your wedding if you so desire. Such specialty services include cake, candles, flowers, centerpieces, printed menus, place cards, table numbers, additional décor, linens, wedding cameras, and table favors. Champagne brunch is also available for opening presents the day after your wedding or for a shower.

World's Fair Pavilion

In Forest Park | St. Louis, Missouri 63110 | 314 289 5344
www.stlouis.missouri.org
Capacity: Up to 500 guests | Rental fee: $700 to $1,400
Cost: Depends on caterer

World's Fair Pavilion, the famous open-air shelter located in Forest Park, is one of the park's most admired attractions. It's a lovely place to have a ceremony or a reception, especially for larger parties. All food and beverages, linens, china, and so forth to be served at World's Fair Pavilion must be provided by a company from their authorized caterer's list. For an unforgettable night in Forest Park, this is a perfect choice. (See Chapter 1, "Ceremonies and Officiants," for more information.)

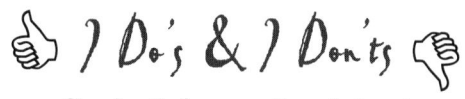

👍 7 Do's & 7 Don'ts 👎

- Check with the reception site to set up a food-tasting appointment.

- Plan a visit on a night the site is set for another wedding to preview reception setup. You could also ask to see photos of the setup.

- Play close attention to the background sound on the night of preview to avoid the noise overpowering speeches and announcements.

- Match your venue size to the number of guests to avoid overcrowding or sparseness. Beware of venues pushing to sell you rooms not suitable for your number of guests.

- Never pay your entire bill up front, and pay with a credit card when allowed to protect yourself in case of any problems.

- Remember to consider the season when choosing an outdoor location and plan an alternate location in case of inclement weather.

- Keep in mind, the venue "rental fee" is a set price and the "cost" is the price per guest.

Notes

Notes

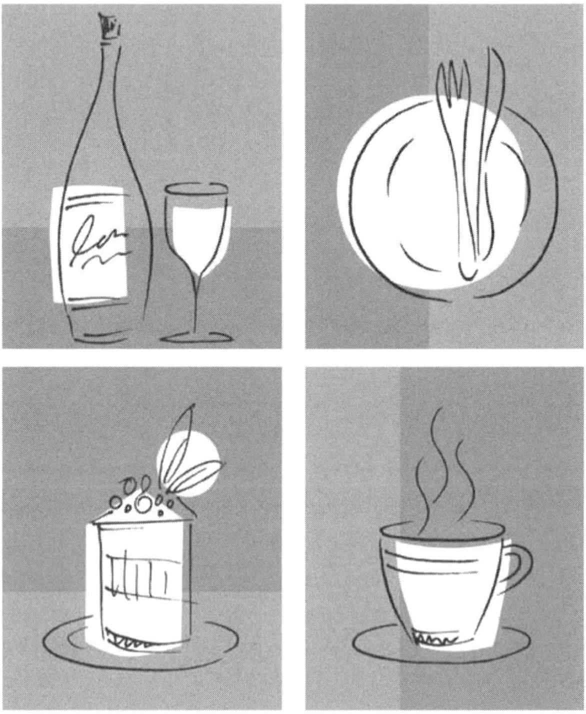

3. Catering

Adding to the tone of your wedding, catering consists of anything or everything from hors d'oeuvres to desserts. Catering may be handled by your reception venue or you may need to choose your own. Some venues only allow you to choose your caterer from their preferred caterers list. If you use your own caterer, plan on spending around 40 percent of your total wedding budget for the service. In this case, you'll use significantly less of your total budget for your reception venue. The main advantages to hiring your own caterer are that you can choose your own type of food or your favorite restaurant.

One disadvantage to having your own caterer is that usually you have to rent your own tables, chairs, linens, china, and glassware. Most catering services offer these and other rentals and services for an additional cost per person, with the exception of tables. Tables and tablecloths are priced per table. In St. Louis, we've found that china and glassware from our preferred caterers will run you around $3.00–$16.00 per person, chairs $3–$10, chair covers $1–$5, tables $50–$250 (some include linens; other don't), and linens $8–$15 per table. Because of all these variables, our cost key only includes average food and bar cost per person on a Saturday night.

Timeline

9 – 12 months
- Interview and choose your caterer.

3 – 6 months
- Meet with caterer for a tasting of cuisine.
- Finalize the menu with your caterer.
- Complete the guest list for a headcount.

2 months
- Update headcount and confirm menu.

1 month
- Finalize and confirm details with caterer.
- Call any guests that haven't responded.

1 – 2 weeks
- Final confirmation to caterer.
- Give final headcount to caterer.

I Do's & I Don'ts

- It's helpful if the caterer you choose has already catered events at your reception location. That way they will know the most successful ways to serve.

- Most caterers will accommodate guests with special dietary needs; all you have to do is ask.

- If you are opting for a cocktail and hors d'oeuvres reception, make sure you note that on the invitation. You don't want guests skipping out early because they are hungry.

- Most of your guests will remember the food more than what color the bridesmaids' dresses are, so if possible, don't be skimpy here.

Money-Saving Tips

- Opt for an hors d'oeuvres or dessert and champagne-only reception versus a dinner.

- Consider other times besides dinner, such as brunch, lunch, or late evening, to hold your reception.

- Check pricing around town for rental items to be sure renting from your catering company is the best deal.

- As always, off-season prices are generally cheaper.

- Think minimal. Guests usually eat light at weddings anyway, so cut back on the number of courses.

- Call in favors from family and friends for a do-it-yourself reception.

Questions to Ask Your Caterer

- What's included in the pricing? Linens, tables, chairs, china, glassware, silverware?
- Is the pricing all-inclusive or is it per item? (Request a menu with pricing if it's not available on their website.)
- How involved are you in the reception? Will you serve as a coordinator during the reception?
- Do you provide cakes, too?
- Will you allow an outside bakery?
- Will you still cut the cake if we opt for an outside bakery?
- Do you provide tastings?
- How many waitstaff do you provide? How are they dressed?

Cost Key

$	under $30
$$	$30 – $50
$$$	$51 – $70
$$$$	$71 – $90
$$$$$	over $90

Butler's Pantry

1414 Park Avenue | St. Louis, Missouri 63104
314 664 7680
www.butlerspantry.com
Cost: $$

Privately owned since 1966, Butler's Pantry offers gorgeous presentation at such venues as the Magic House, City Museum, Piper Palm House, and Mad Art. This awarding-winning caterer is exclusive to the Piper Palm House located in Tower Grove Park. Besides buffet and sit-down options, they offer delectable specialty stations such as seafood or vegetarian. Prices are based on 100 guests minimum.

Catering St. Louis

2141 59th Street | St. Louis, Missouri 63110
314 961 7588
www.cateringstlouis.com
Cost: $$$

Catering St. Louis prides itself on excellent service. There is no service too minuscule or too extravagant for them to handle. They regularly cater all of the Forest Park venues as well as the Botanical Garden and many other famous sites around town. Besides the buffet and seated dinners, for a more affordable option hors d'oeuvres receptions are offered. Prices are based on 55 guests minimum.

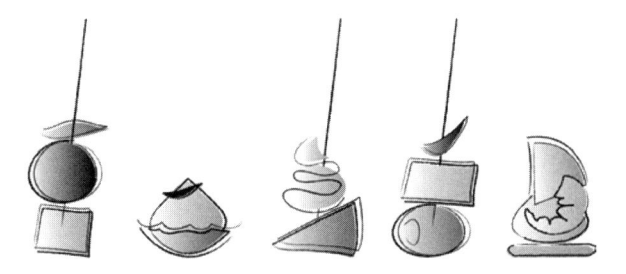

Cuisine d'Art

701 N. New Ballas Road | Creve Coeur, Missouri 63141
(café location)
314 995 3003
www.cuisine-dart.com
Cost: $$-$$$$$

We first heard about Cuisine d'Art while researching one of our favorite reception sites. Starting as a home-based business, the company has grown over the past 15 years to accommodate 2,000 guests with casual and full-service catering. They also have a bakery and café in Creve Coeur. With such a wide pricing range, they can accommodate most any budget.

Gregory's Creative Cuisine

4700 Adkins Avenue | St. Louis, Missouri 63116
314 481 4481
www.gregoryscreativecuisine.com
Cost: $-$$$

Owner and executive chef Gregory Mosberger has been serving St. Louis for more than 16 years. Allison first discovered this caterer when she lived near Bevo Mill in South City. What stood out to us were Gregory's choices in the type of menus he has available. For example, he offers healthy hors d'oeuvres, themed meals, and a "Best for Less" dinner entrée, which is great for couples on a budget. They offer gourmet food and limitless choices at an affordable price.

Hendri's Banquets and Catering

4501 Ridgewood Avenue | St. Louis, Missouri 63116
314 752 4084
www.hendris.com
Cost: $$

Because Hendri's is also one of our favorite reception sites, we'll cut right to the chase. Emily was in a wedding at Hendri's and the experience confirmed our affections for this food and venue. As with most caterers, china, glassware, tables, and linens are priced separately. Hendri's regularly caters Casa Loma Ballroom, Mahler Ballroom, Powell Symphony Hall, Sheldon Ballroom, Tower Grove Park, and many other venues around town.

LaChef & Co.

7169 Manchester Road | St. Louis, Missouri 63143
314 647 5350
www.lachef.com
Cost: $$-$$$

Owned and operated by Sherrill Gonterman for more than 25 years, LaCHEF & Co. caters such venues as COCA, The Magic House, The Studio at St. Albans, The Jewel Box, Powell Symphony Hall, and Mt. Pleasant Winery, to name a few. They also offer 26 specialty stations, such as a burger bar, pasta bar, shrimp or sushi bars, and dessert martini bar. Prices are based on 30 guests minimum.

Patty Long Catering

1804 S. Ninth Street | St. Louis, Missouri 63104
314 621 9598
www.pattylongcatering.com
Cost: $$$

Patty Long Catering has been named St. Louis' best caterer countless times over the past 20 years. They cater such venues as the Ninth Street Abbey, the City Museum, the History Museum, and many more. Some of our favorite specialty stations of their twelve offered are St. Louis barbecue, Asian, Southwest, Greek, and the mashed potato bar. Prices are based on 50 guests minimum.

Russo's Gourmet Catering

9904 Page Avenue | St. Louis, Missouri 63132
314 427 6771
www.russosgourmet.com
Cost: $$-$$$

Russo's has been catering St. Louis for more than 50 years. They have three exclusive facilities where they offer all-inclusive packages: Graphic Arts Banquet Center, Spazio's (featured in Chapter 2, "Receptions"), and Xavier Grand Ballroom. Russo's also offers some enhancements to make your event more memorable such as frozen drink machines, tents, arcade/casino games, and themed props. Prices are based on 150 guests minimum.

Notes

Notes

Music

4. Music

Generally speaking, about 10 percent of your wedding budget should be set aside for music. Music and entertainment is what Emily and I remember most about the past weddings that we have attended. We don't usually recall the favors given or the bridesmaids' dress colors unless they were particularly unusual. But music adds so much to your special day. It creates moods by making people smile and cry, and it gets everyone out of their seats to party.

You will likely want music both at the ceremony and at the reception. There are many choices to consider. Do you want a string quartet or a vocalist at your ceremony? Bagpipes or a pianist? Will the musician be a friend or someone you have hired just for the occasion?

When deciding on the type of music for the reception, think about your style and think about your guests. What will keep everyone entertained the entire night? Would you prefer a live band or a DJ? Also consider matching your entertainment to the style of your wedding. This chapter gives you options of musicians around town that are our favorites based on our extensive interviews.

DJ vs. Band

DJs and bands are the most common entertainers for receptions, so we decided to list some differences to help you choose between them. DJs tend to cost a lot less than a band, ranging from about $500 to $800 for a four- or five-hour reception.

A band in St. Louis will range from $1,500 to $5,000. Band prices vary by the number of musicians. Live music adds a special touch to the reception, but DJs have more of a variety of music.

General Questions to Ask Any Musician

- Do you have a demo tape or can we see you perform live?
- Are you familiar with our site?
- What fees will be charged? What kind of deposit is required?
- What is the overtime charge?
- What equipment are we expected to provide?
- How much space is needed?
- How much setup time is needed?
- What will the musicians' attire consist of?
- Will we be expected to provide meals and beverages?
- What happens if a musician or DJ is unable to play at the reception, as in case of an emergency?
- How far in advance do we need to sign a contract?
- Do you have liability insurance?
- What is the cancellation/refund policy?

) Do's &) Don'ts

- All music acts, including DJs, can book up quickly especially if they are popular and in high demand. Plan on booking nine months to a year in advance.

- If you are hiring a musician (or musicians) for your ceremony, check with the officiant for your service first: some sites have strict guidelines about which music can and can't be played during a ceremony.

- Consider the size of the ceremony site when choosing your music so that your music is heard but not overwhelming. A quintet may be too loud in a very small chapel, yet a flutist at a huge winery with a very large crowd may not reach everyone's ears.

- Make sure there is ample space for either a DJ or a band at the reception. Some venues don't offer much space for an eight-piece band, for example.

- Visit the DJ or band in action if you can. You will want to pay attention to the way they dress, how the crowd is reacting, and most important, the music.

- It is always good to book a band that performs for weddings, not just in bars and nightclubs. A band that performs at weddings has to hold the audience's attention for five or six hours whereas a band at a nightclub has a changing audience every one or two hours.

- If hiring a band, make some CDs comprising your favorite songs to play during breaks.

- Give your DJ or band music requests that indicate the music you want and do not want. You don't want your guests doing the Electric Slide, for example, if you don't dig the song.

- The entertainers you hire are much more than simply a source of music. They are also your emcee for the night, making each and every announcement, so provide details such as the names of your wedding party for introductions and the timeline of how the night is planned.

- And don't forget, book your entertainment well in advance!

The Chesterfield Quartet

314 469 3432
www.chesterfieldquartet.com
Cost: Wedding ceremony – $429
Wedding ceremony and 1-hour reception – $629
Wedding ceremony and 2-hour reception – $829
Reception (1-hour minimum):
1st hour – $399 | 2nd hour – $200 | 3rd hour – $200
Trumpet soloist (subject to availability) – $150
Other instrumental soloist(s) – varies
Vocal soloist (for full Mass, includes 3 songs and all the Eucharistic responses to the Mass) – $150
Vocal soloist (3-song minimum) – $40 per song

Timeline

9 – 12 months
- Interview and choose your entertainment.

2 months
- Give your live band any requested songs they might need to learn.

1 month
- Finalize and confirm details with the entertainment.

1 – 2 weeks
- Final confirmation with the entertainment.
- Provide a song list to your musicians or DJ detailing songs you want and don't want played. Include song requests.

The Chesterfield Quartet was recommended by good friends of ours, Bryan and Tanya. They had the quartet play at their wedding ceremony and loved them. Bryan and Tanya said they were easy to work with and sounded fabulous. Their guests even mentioned how lovely the quartet played. The Chesterfield Quartet has been performing in St. Louis since 1985 and is famous for playing at wedding ceremonies and receptions. They have a collection of music with more than 700 compositions, including classical, jazz, and show tunes.

Complete Music

11224 Olive Boulevard | St. Louis, Missouri 63141
314 991 5656
www.completemusicinc.com
Cost: Packages start at $595

Complete Music was voted the number one DJ service in North America by *Entrepreneur* and *Success* magazine. They have been in business for more than 25 years and are "the industry's most experienced company" around, according to their website. Complete Music is not only a DJ service but also an entertainment service. Their top priority is making the guests smile, and each DJ is trained and experienced to do so. Whether you are having a formal or informal reception, the DJs know how to entertain your crowd. They can initiate participation dances, provide children's activities during dinner, and even offer balloon art and magic. When you book a Complete Music DJ, you get a reception planner, an emcee, and an entertainer. They also offer video services. (See Chapter 6, "Videography.")

Harp Inspirations

636 225 8548
www.harpinspirations.com
Cost: Call for pricing

Sue Druckenmiller is a freelance harpist who established Harp Inspirations because she wanted to share her gift of music with others for special occasions. She says she absolutely loves to play the harp and considers it more than a job. She has a large song collection including classical, romantic, easy listening, and Celtic songs to choose from and adds new selections every year. Her wedding package includes the consultation, transporting the harp, setting up, tuning, half hour of prelude music, ceremony music, and about ten to fifteen minutes of postlude. Weather permitting, Sue will even play outdoors. Please check out her website to hear samples from her latest CD. Sue says that she has always been successful and has many references if needed.

Jukebox Productions

636 939 6410
http://jukeboxproductions.homestead.com
Cost: Rates start at $450 for 4 hours, plus $75 for each additional hour. Discount rates available for events held at select banquet facilities and volume bookings

Jukebox Productions was started by Gary and Kimberly Williams back in 1987. Gary was a musician who played in bands for more than 18 years, but in 1987 he decided to create an entertaining mobile DJ company. Each and every DJ with Jukebox Productions is also an entertainer—either a musician of some sort or a dancer, which can add a special touch to your reception. They offer a wide range of music, from the 1930s to hip hop. They even offer your Latin favorites. Packages begin at four hours with an additional charge for longer events. Jukebox Productions also offers dance lessons in their studio, which might be an idea to consider since you will be dancing in front of dozens of friends and family. In addition, if you are a Karaoke kind of couple, they offer the equipment to add to your package.

Questions to ask a DJ or Band for a Reception

- Does the DJ or band have experience with wedding receptions? How long have they been performing at receptions?
- Will the DJ or band leader also act as the emcee, making announcements and so forth?
- Can we meet with the actual DJ or band leader that will be our entertainer?
- Does the band charge a flat fee or is it per musician?
- Do you take requests? Will you accept "want" and "do not want" song lists?
- Do you interact with the audience at all?
- Will the band or musician learn a particular song of our choice? What will the fee be?

Spectrum Band

314 434 7153
www.spectrumband.net
Cost: Reception packages range from $1,800 to $3,000
Ceremony packages start at $150

The Spectrum Band is a nine-piece band that can play a variety of genres of music, including swing, R&B, Motown, pop, jazz, and '50s and '60s. They were recently voted Best Band in Missouri by *Modern Bride* magazine. We contacted the bandleader, Tim Callihan, who is also the drummer and percussionist, and he was very helpful. The instrumentation of Spectrum Band consists of a female and male lead vocalist, guitar, bass, saxophone, trumpet, keyboards, and drums for a complete diverse sound. They also use a trombone, harmonica, and Latin percussion instruments during their performances. If you are not interested in an eight-piece band, they also offer three- and four-piece bands for smaller events. Their website is full of video clips, samples of their music, and tons of information.

TKO DJs

7434 Manchester Road | St. Louis, Missouri 63143
314 647 3000
www.tko-djs.com
Cost: Call for pricing

TKO DJs have been entertaining crowds at receptions for more than 25 years. Each DJ is professional and experienced and will have all of your guests up on the dance floor the entire night. They have one of the biggest music selections with more than 40,000 titles and have great sound and light equipment. Whether you are looking for a DJ to interact with the audience and organize special dances or want one to sit back and just play your favorite tunes, TKO DJs has what you're looking for.

The Ultraviolets

314 610 9842
www.theultraviolets.net
Cost: Call for pricing

The Ultraviolets are the band Paulo and Emily contracted for their reception. We can't say enough good things about them. The lead vocalist, Linda Gaal, worked with Paulo and Emily, and they originally heard them at the company holiday party. Then they kept hearing them play at Harry's downtown and fell in love with their music. Keep in mind, the Ultraviolets will book up at least a year in advance. Their five-piece band plays an array of music including Motown, disco, funk, classic rock, '80s dance, modern rock, hip hop, and pop favorites. If you have a song in mind that they don't know, they will learn it before your reception. That was what impressed Paulo and Emily most. They had a couple of songs that the band didn't know and the Ultraviolets learned them for the event. In between their few breaks, they have a full sound system that will play any music you want. Additionally, their microphones and PA are available for announcements, and they will come dressed to impress. The Ultraviolets are great to work with and we highly recommend them for a live band. They will amaze your guests and get them moving!

Notes

64 Photography

5. Photography

Picking your photographer is probably one of the most crucial decisions you will make throughout the whole wedding planning process. Photographers will take about 10 percent of your wedding budget, but for most couples, it is well worth it. Wedding photos are a lasting keepsake of your wedding and you will treasure them for the rest of your life.

First you will need to decide which type of photography fits your style. Photographers generally fall into one of three categories: traditional or formal, photojournalistic or candid, and a mix of both. If you prefer more classic "posed" pictures, choose a traditional photographer. If you prefer more candid, fun, non-traditional shots, lean toward a photojournalistic photographer. If you can't decide or like both types, choose a photographer who enjoys both. In this chapter, we included our favorite photographers around St. Louis to satisfy everyone's taste and budget.

Do's & Don'ts

Timeline

12 – 18 months
- Interview and choose your photographer.

1 month
- Finalize and confirm details with the photographer including a list of your must-have shots.

1 – 2 weeks
- Final confirmation with your photographer.

- Check out the photographer's website and browse through galleries before going to meet him or her. It will give you a good idea about the type and style of photography each one offers and will save you time.

- Make sure you meet the actual photographer who will shoot your special day.

- Make sure your style matches up with his or hers. For example, if you really dig black-and-white photos, make sure that's included in the package.

- Make a list of any special photos you definitely want your photographer to capture. For example, you might want a photo of you and your girlfriends from your old neighborhood. Be sure to communicate your list with your photographer.

- Make sure you get along with your photographer because you are going to be spending a long hectic day with him or her. If you are not getting a good vibe from the person, even if you like the photos and he or she seems affordable, look again for another photographer. It is not worth having an entire album with fake smiles.

- Be sure to get references from the photographer you choose. If he or she is reputable, the photographer will be happy to offer references to you.

Artisan Photography

760 Penny Court | Ballwin, Missouri 63011
636 207 7883
www.stlphotography.com
Cost: Packages start at $3,000

Timothy Pastor, owner and creator of Artisan Photography, adds his artistic touch to each of his photos. He will capture every moment of your wedding day in a journalistic view that will be cherished all your life. The price of his packages includes the wedding day photography and the album. If you are looking for something artistic and journalistic, Artisan Photography would be perfect! Check out the galleries on their website; they are amazing!

Chris Croy Photography

12834 Canterbury Farms Drive | St. Louis, Missouri 63128
314 842 3980
www.chriscroy.com
Cost: Call for pricing

Chris Croy and his group of photographers are sincerely artists. Check out the galleries on their website or stop by the studio to thumb through some portfolios and albums to see their talent. With the experience of shooting more than 700 weddings, they can tailor their photography to any bride and groom and catch all the emotions to design an ideal album. By being familiar with most venues and churches in the St. Louis area, they have an eye for picking the most striking locations with perfect lighting and gorgeous settings. Most packages include two photographers to catch every moment and assemble a "storylike" album for the couple to cherish the rest of their lives.

CLC Photography

2910 Macklind Avenue | St. Louis, Missouri 63139
314 647 8300
www.clcphoto.com
Cost: Packages start at $3,000

Christopher L. Cook, owner of CLC Photography, uses a "documentary-style" approach with his exceptional and imaginative views. He prefers to keep posed photos to a minimum and have more artistic portraits for the bride and groom. Chris obtains a laid-back style of wedding photography and settles in the background to capture all the right moments and emotions while putting the bride and groom at ease. Check out the photo galleries on his website to get a feel for his special touch.

Memories Are Forever

1568 Ross Avenue | St. Louis, Missouri 63146
314 878 5657
www.memoriesareforever.com
Cost: Packages start at $1,849
Special pricing for The Conservatory (Packages starting at $499)

Memories Are Forever concentrates on both formal portraits and photojournalistic-style photography in both black-and-white and color. Most of their packages have no hourly rate or time limitation and the photographers set no limit on the number of photographs they need to take to capture your special day. Visit their website where you can search by location or by photographer. Believe us, you will be impressed!

Nordmann Photography

7714 Big Bend | Shrewsbury, Missouri 63119
314 783 0300
www.nordmannphoto.com
Cost: Call for pricing

Nordmann Photography was the photographer that Emily chose for her wedding. They were recommended by someone Emily worked with at the time, and she couldn't have been happier. Nordmann's wedding photos have been featured in *St. Louis Bride*, *The Knot*, *St. Louis Best Bridal*, and *St. Louis Bride and Groom*. Their photographers have a very journalistic view, which matched Paulo and Emily's style exactly. Not to mention they were very easy and fun to work with during the whole process. Nordmann Photography focuses both on illustrative and journalistic designs. Their collections include both black-and-white and color photos, the album, all the photos in the album, an image catalogue (proofs), and a website where family and friends can view and purchase photos.

P.S. Tim Nordmann, son of the owner, specializes in video. He was Emily's videographer and was impressive.
See Chapter 6, "Videography."

Money-Saving Tips

- Limit your time with the photographer to cut costs. Maybe have him or her take formal pictures at the ceremony only.

- Hire a photographer who will give you the digital files. That way you can print copies at another time.

- Have a friend, family member, or amateur take pictures.

Signature Studio

1006 Olive Street, Ste. 301 | St. Louis, MO 63101 | 314 241 7555
100 Chesterfield Business Parkway, Ste. 200 | Chesterfield, MO 63005
636 681 1445
www.signaturestudio.com
Cost: Packages start at $2,700

Signature Studio is owned by award-winning artistic photographer Pam Bredenkamp. Pam is a true St. Louisan, but she lived briefly in California so she adds a California twist to her art. Pam and Signature Studio receive outstanding reviews from brides and grooms. The couples say she has a great personality and they think of her as a friend. Signature Studio shoots formal or photojournalistic photos, black-and-white or color; it is up to the bride and groom. They please all generations and create albums describing each moment and emotion of the entire special day. They specialize in award-winning photography and wedding album design.

Snapshot Photography

314 221 8548
www.snapshotphoto.smugmug.com
Cost: Packages start at $75

Karen Creager, owner of Snapshot Photography and more importantly our mom, is a fantastic, affordable option for smaller weddings. Packages include 1-5 hours and a password-protected portfolio online with option to purchase customized photo packages. CDs also available for an additional fee. She offers photojournalistic and traditional style specializing in engagement photos and parties, wedding showers, and rehearsal dinners with packages starting at $75. It must be written that she comes with our highest recommendation and guarantee!

St. Louis Color, Inc.

9909 Clayton Road, Suite LL-10 | Ladue, Missouri 63124
314 997 1505
www.journalisticstyle.com
Cost: Packages start at $600

St. Louis Color has a wide range of talented photographers ready to capture each important aspect of your wedding day and create an amazing album to remember. All of their artistic photographers will shoot formal and candid (journalistic) pictures, according to your style. They can even do both styles to complete a photographic story of your big day! St. Louis Color packages are well suited for any individual. You may get a package based on the level of service you are looking for. If you want a huge portion of your wedding budget spent on a photographer consider choosing a Senior Photographer to photograph your event. If you are trying to cut costs a little, you may choose a basic package. Or if you want something in between, opt for an Associate Photographer. They also offer a number of specials. Take a look at their website to view each photographer's background and work as well as many different ceremony and reception locations around the St. Louis area.

For free or minimal fee try **kizoa.com**, **smilebox.com**, **slideroll.com**, or **photoshow.com** to make a free slideshow of photos to show at your rehearsal dinner, wedding, or reception.

Susan Jackson Photography

2519 Mentor Place | St. Louis, Missouri 63144 | 314 918 8400
www.susanjacksonphoto.com
Cost: Call for pricing

Susan Jackson Photography has some of the most astounding photography that we have seen in St. Louis. Susan has been a photographer for more than 11 years now, but you would think it has been a lifetime. She has a widespread background in graphic design and is highly experienced in fashion photography. These combined can create miracles. Her work has appeared in *Martha Stewart Weddings*, *Glamour Magazine*, and more. Friends of ours used her for their wedding and were impressed with the whole package. They said her work is phenomenal and it was a pleasure to do business with her. Susan's website states that her expertise makes her "one of the most sought-after wedding photojournalists in the country."

T. Kratzer Photography

O'Fallon, Missouri 63366 | 636 240 6380 or 314 707 1655
www.tkratzerphoto.com
Cost: Packages start at $1,750

Tracy Kratzer has been serving St. Louis since 1987 with a great deal of experience in wedding photography. She focuses on both traditional and photojournalistic shooting. While writing this book we researched many St. Louis wedding message boards and just about every person has raved about Tracy's work. Brides mention her affordable prices, her high-quality work, and how great and easy it is to do business with her. She offers traditional, classic, and deluxe packages and can mix and match each style of photography, fitting each bride's individual needs.

Trotter Photo

14319 Manchester Road | Manchester, MO 63011 | 636 394 7689
8471 Mexico Road | St. Peters, Missouri 63376 | 636 978 7689
431 Dunn Road | Florissant, Missouri 63031 | 314 921 9494
2177 Lone Star Drive | Arnold, Missouri 63010 | 636 296 6767
www.trotterphoto.com
Cost: Packages start at $475

Trotter Photo has been serving St. Louis for more than 35 years. They offer many different styles including traditional, photojournalistic, candid, black-and-white, and digital. All their packages include albums and pages. You may also create your own package and combine different styles to your liking. Trotter Photo is very affordable and has a great reputation around St. Louis. Personally, we know many brides and grooms who have chosen Trotter and have heard nothing but good reviews. With four locations around the Saint Louis metro area, you can't go wrong.

Warwick Photography

Office: 9020 Manchester Road | St. Louis, Missouri 63144
Studio: 1750 S. Brentwood Boulevard, Suite 209
           Brentwood, Missouri 63144 | 314 962 3222
www.warwickphotography.com
Cost: Packages start at $1,500

Tom Warwick's extensive background as a newspaper photojournalist, model, and fashion photographer yields him to be a highly requested wedding photographer. Kodak and Fuji consider Tom one of the top 100 talented photographers in the United States. He has also received the Award of Distinction by the International Professional Photographers Hall of Fame. Tom has put together a team of extremely talented individuals who parallel Tom's work because of constant training and learning. Each wedding package is custom designed to fit the couple's needs and wants. In addition, each album is tailored to match the style and personality of the bride and groom. To catch a glimpse of his work, step inside the studio in Brentwood to see a complete audio-visual presentation. You will be amazed.

Questions to Ask Your Photographer

- What is your primary style of photography?
- Do you shoot in color, black-and-white, or both? Does it cost extra to have black-and-white or to do both?
- Can we tell you ahead of time what shots we definitely want, or do you pick every shot?
- Are you the person who will actually take our pictures? If not, can we meet the person who will be?
- Can we meet any of the assistants who will be helping out taking pictures?
- How many weddings have you photographed? How many similar to the size and formality of our wedding?
- Do you have any references (people who have used their services for their wedding) that I can contact?
- How many other weddings will you also photograph the weekend of our wedding?
- Do we receive the negatives or files of the photos or are they available for purchase on a CD?
- How much do you charge if I go over my allotted time? Are there overtime charges?
- Will I be expected to provide beverages or meals for you and your assistants?
- Do you have an emergency photographer substitute plan?
- What is your cancellation and refund policy?
- Are you familiar with our ceremony and reception locations?

Notes

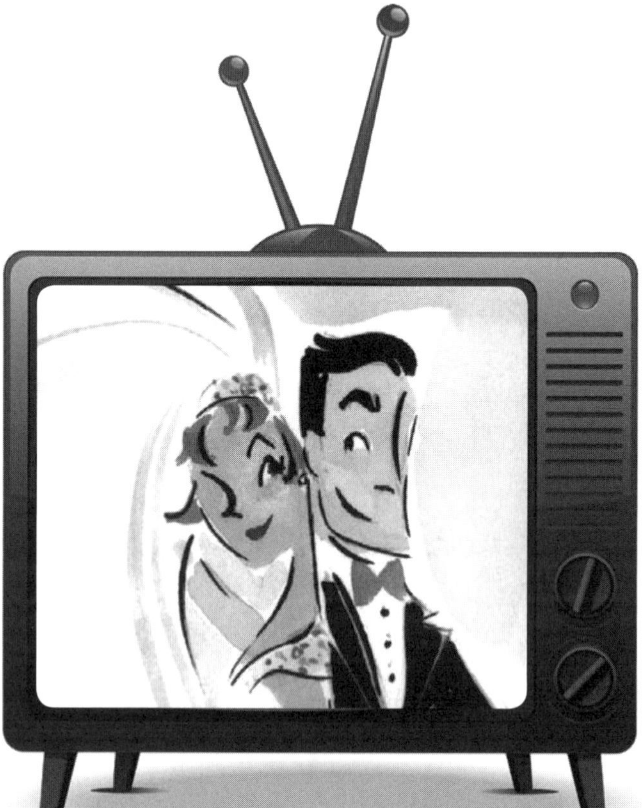

6. Videography

Before you know it, you will be home from your honeymoon and all you will have left is the top tier of your wedding cake in the freezer, a dress that needs to be taken to the cleaners, a few pictures, and a dreamlike memory of the wedding day. When we think back to our wedding day, everything seems like a huge blur. Because of this, many brides consider hiring a videographer to capture every waking moment of their big day. It is a good way for friends and family who could not make it to experience the memories. Your best friend, after one too many cocktails, dancing as if no one is paying attention and the look on your new spouse's face when he or she first sees you coming down the aisle are just two of the priceless moments that only video can capture.

Sometimes brides and grooms try to cut costs by having a family member catch the memories with his or her personal camcorder. Unfortunately, while using a friend might work for still photography, we cannot recommend this for videos. Most likely your video will come back with distorted sound, bad lighting, and the videographer's body parts in view. Plus, the family member or friend won't be able to enjoy the ceremony or reception. Equipment and lighting make all the difference in the world and unless you are working with a professional, you are going to face a nightmare. In this chapter, we include all our preferred videographers from the St. Louis area.

I Do's & I Don'ts

- Book your videographer a year in advance. Most well-known videographers around St. Louis are booked at least that far in advance.
- Create a list of must-have moments and be sure to go over them with the videographer prior to the big day.
- Ask the videographer if he or she has a sample video to view.

Timeline

12 - 18 months
- Interview and choose your videographer.

1 month
- Finalize and confirm details with the videographer including a list of your must-have shots.

1 - 2 weeks
- Final confirmation with your videographer.

Money-Saving Tips

- Pick a package that only includes one video camera with no editing of the footage.
- Limit the number of hours you have the videographer at the ceremony or reception.
- Some photography studios also include videography services. You may be able to get a discount if you purchase photography and videography from the same location.

Questions to Ask Your Videographer

- What is your videography style? Is it straight-shot with no editing, documentary (storylike with interviews), or more artsy (special effects, music, photo clips), or a mix of all three?
- How many weddings have you shot? Do you provide samples? (Make sure you find out whose samples you are seeing. Could be the owner's work but the day of your wedding, the assistant is running the camera.)
- Are you a member of any videography associations? Have you won any awards?
- Do you coordinate with the wedding photographer?
- Have you ever shot a wedding or reception at our site? Do you have samples of video at that venue?
- How many weddings or receptions will you shoot the day of our wedding and reception? How many weddings or receptions do you do a weekend? A year?
- Will you be shooting our wedding or someone else? If not, can we interview the actual videographer?
- How many cameras do you use and what kind of cameras do you use? Are they up-to-date, high-quality cameras?
- What kind of microphones do you provide? Wireless?
- What type of lighting do you use?
- Will I be expected to provide beverages or meals for you and your assistants?
- Do you have backup equipment in case of emergency?
- What is your cancellation/refund policy?

Complete Video

11224 Olive Boulevard | St. Louis, Missouri 63141
314 991 5656
www.completemusicinc.com
Cost: Packages start at $995

Complete Video offers a wide range of packages to fit each couple's budget. Check out the demo videos on their website.

Kevin Harder Videography

4592 Braungate Drive | St. Louis, Missouri 63128
314 894 3311
www.kevinhardervideo.com
Cost: Packages start at $750

Kevin Harder has been filming special events for more than 25 years and specializes in weddings. He and his team of about 10 talented videographers film more than 150 weddings each year and they keep growing. Kevin offers many different types of packages depending on each bride and groom's needs and wants.

Lifetime Media

8140 Brentwood Industrial Drive | St. Louis, Missouri 63144
314 481 4754
www.lifetime-media.com
Cost: Call for pricing

Lifetime Media is a unique videography service that stood out to us while visiting bridal shows around St. Louis. Their staff has more than 30 years of combined experience in the business and is extremely creative and professional. Lifetime Media offers three different wedding packages to fit the needs of any bride or groom, including the Simple Plan, the Production Plan, and the Vignettes.

New Directions Media

6209 Mid Rivers Mall Drive, Ste. 300 | St. Charles, Missouri 63304
888 298 7436
www.newdirectionsmedia.com
Cost: Packages start at $799

New Directions Media makes every effort to create an innovative and unique approach to wedding videography. With the latest technology, they are able to capture every mood or emotion that is visible throughout your special day. They offer a variety of packages based on your budget. Some options include a growing-up photo montage, love story, rehearsal highlights, 360° panoramic images, and even a honeymoon photo montage.

Nordmann Productions

7714 Big Bend | Shrewsbury, Missouri 63119
314 783 0300
www.nordmannproductions.com
Cost: Call for pricing

Emily and Paulo chose Nordmann Productions for their videography. One reason they chose them was that their photographers, Nordmann Photography, recommended the owner's son, Tim Nordmann. He was wonderful to work with. Known as one of St. Louis' finest wedding videographers, Tim has a photojournalistic style that creates a video of art you will cherish forever. His packages include engagement stories, post-wedding interviews, and interviews by other members of the wedding party, which all add special touches to your wedding video. Visit the Nordmann Productions website to watch some of their wedding videos.

Video Vantages

St. Louis, Missouri 63146
314 994 3123
www.videovantages.com
Cost: Packages start at $795

Video Vantages is owned and operated by Gert Booher. Allison and Brian chose Video Vantages for their wedding back in August of 2001 and were very pleased. What Allison likes best about Gert's work is that she is very easy to work with, offers affordable packages, and really focuses on getting every moment on tape. She even stayed to the very end of the reception to catch Allison's brother-in-law, Matt, in action performing the air guitar. Gert has been capturing treasured wedding memories on video since 1990 and has a real knack for it. She offers several different packages, including a "No-Edit" special of three and a half to four hours of raw footage for brides and grooms on a budget. She also offers love stories, music videos, highlights, and photo montages, and she is open to any requests.

Notes

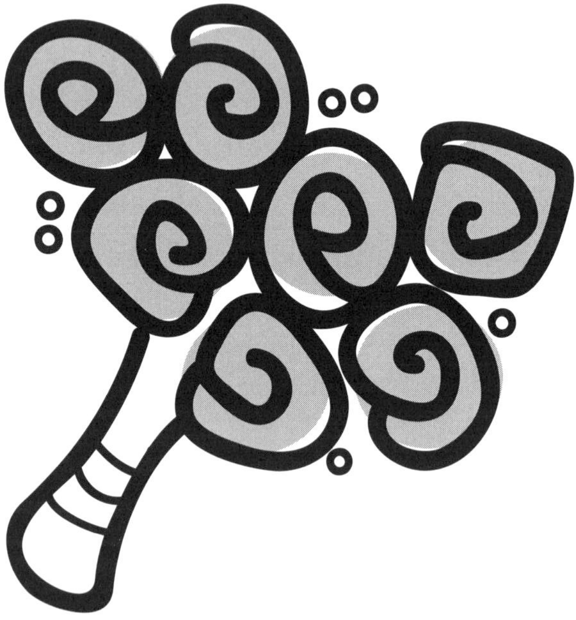

7. Flowers

Choosing a florist in St. Louis can be a daunting task. There are more than 10 pages of florists to choose from in the phone book, so it's overwhelming when you are trying to figure out where to start. Lucky for you, we have sorted through them and feature only those that impressed us most!

Begin by allocating 8–10 percent of your budget toward flowers. When you meet with a florist, it is helpful to bring pictures of ideas (colors, flower choice, arrangement style), a picture or swatch of your bridesmaid dresses, price quotes from other florists, and lists of arrangements you will need and who they are for.

Some basic uses of flowers include ceremony décor; reception centerpieces; bride's, maid of honor, and bridesmaids' bouquets; corsages for mothers and grandmothers; boutonnieres for groomsmen, ring bearer, fathers, and grandfathers; and petals for the flower girl. Other arrangements you might consider are for your cake, cake table, guest book table, garland, flower girl's head dress, and flower girl basket.

👍 Do's & Don'ts 👎

- Secure your ceremony and reception sites first and determine the colors that you are using for your wedding.
- Bring ideas and questions to your appointment with the florist.
- Most florists will show you samples and maybe even offer to show you a wedding or reception already decorated. Use this opportunity to decide whether your styles match.
- Don't go overboard—especially in ornate settings such as churches or outdoors.

Timeline

6 – 9 months
- Interview and choose your florist.

3 – 6 months
- Order flowers

1 month
- Finalize and confirm details with the florist.

1 – 2 weeks
- Final confirmation with your florist.

💰 Money-Saving Tips

- Caution when scheduling during holidays: Flowers in demand mean higher prices especially during Valentine's Day weekend and Mother's Day weekend.
- Choose flowers that are in season for lower prices.
- Take a seminar and design your own floral arrangements.
- Limit the number of arrangements.

Questions to Ask Your Florist

- Are my preferred flowers in season? What flowers are in season during my wedding date?
- What are the average prices for my choices of flowers?
- How many floral designers do you have?
- Which designers did which arrangements in your portfolio?
- What happens if the designer I choose leaves your company before my wedding?
- How far before the wedding do you work on the arrangements?
- Do you charge for delivery? Setup?
- Do you have rental supplies?
- (If your location is out of this area) Do you have a limit on how far you will travel to a location?
- Are you familiar with my ceremony and reception locations?
- If needed, will you transport ceremony decorations to the reception?
- Can you give me an itemized quote?
- How far in advance do I need to secure a date? What do you need from me in order to secure my date?
- What is the average cost of wedding flowers for your clients?
- What is your refund and cancellation policy?
- What is the deposit? Will I get the deposit back or do you subtract it from the final cost?
- May I make partial payments? When is the final payment due? Is gratuity included?

Don DeFoe's Flowers

10212 Watson Road | St. Louis, Missouri 63127
314 966 2461
www.dondefoe.com
Cost: Bridal bouquet – $35 and up
Centerpiece – $20 and up

Family owned since 1962, Don DeFoe's Flowers has four designers including an FTD Master Designer. This FTD florist offers affordable arrangements with a variety of flowers and styles to choose from including custom arrangements. Because they are an FTD florist many of the prices are listed online to give you a good idea for your budget, but they'll design custom arrangements as well. Allison used Don DeFoe's for her wedding (it was included in her reception's wedding package—Holiday Inn Southwest). She brought in pictures and ideas of the bouquets and arrangements she wanted, and the friendly staff worked with her to make the exact type of arrangement she was looking for at a great price.

Elegant Celebrations

629 N. New Ballas Road, #208 | St. Louis, Missouri 63141
314 993 1717
www.elegantcelebrationsstl.com
Cost: Call for pricing

Trisha Haisler, owner and floral designer of Elegant Celebrations, has 20 years of experience, and her attractive arrangements are a reflection. Her style ranges from classic and classy to contemporary and creative. She's been a member of the American Institute of Floral Designers since 1997 and teaches floral design at Southwestern Illinois College (SWIC).

Fresh Art, LLC

7639 Wydown Boulevard | Clayton, Missouri 63105
314 721 5080
www.freshartllc.com
Cost: Bridal bouquets – $150 and up
Centerpieces – $250 and up

Allison's personal favorite, Ardell Burchard is the owner and floral designer of Fresh Art, LLC. Her brilliant use of color, texture, and design are a few of the reasons she's been featured in *Better Homes Magazine*, *Martha Stewart*, *St. Louis Seasons* (twice), and *St. Louis Bride* (twice), and on the cover of *Ladue News*. Although her main focus is weddings, she also designs arrangements for corporate events including those at Washington University and Art in Bloom at the St. Louis Art Museum for the past four years. We love how she uses a variety of flowers and arrangements for weddings with the colors and textures meshing beautifully. View her portfolio online.

Les Bouquets

828 Carmen Woods Road | Manchester, Missouri 63021
636 346 4927
www.lesbouquets.com
Cost: Bridal bouquet – $75 to $275
Centerpieces – $25 and up

Melinda Roeleveld, owner and flower designer, fell in love with flowers after living in Europe for more than 15 years. She states on her website, "I desire to create artistic, unique, quality floral designs for every budget and I take the time to think through ideas (draw lots of sketches) that fit my clients' personality and style. That alone is an art in itself, but I love the challenge of serving my customers the best I can." Take a look at her portfolio online and call her for a free consultation.

Petals Galore

314 651 1360
www.petalsgalore.com
Cost: Call for pricing

The contemporary explosions of color and design make Petals Galore another great choice of florist. They've been featured in such publications as *In Style Weddings*, *St. Louis Brides*, and *St. Charles Magazine*, as well as on *Show Me St. Louis* and KYKY 98.1 FM radio. They offer a wide variety of beautiful flowers and styles from brightly colored hand-tied bouquets to sophisticated nosegays.

Sisters Flowers & Gifts

511 Central Place | St. Louis, Missouri 63122
314 821 0076
www.sistersflowers.net
Cost: Bridal bouquet – $95 and up
Bridesmaid bouquets – $20 and up
Centerpieces – $25 and up

Sisters Flowers & Gifts offers fresh, simple, elegant arrangements with a variety of choices to fit your budget. From classic to contemporary designs, there is something to fit your style and still fall within your price range. Check out their portfolios online.

Notes

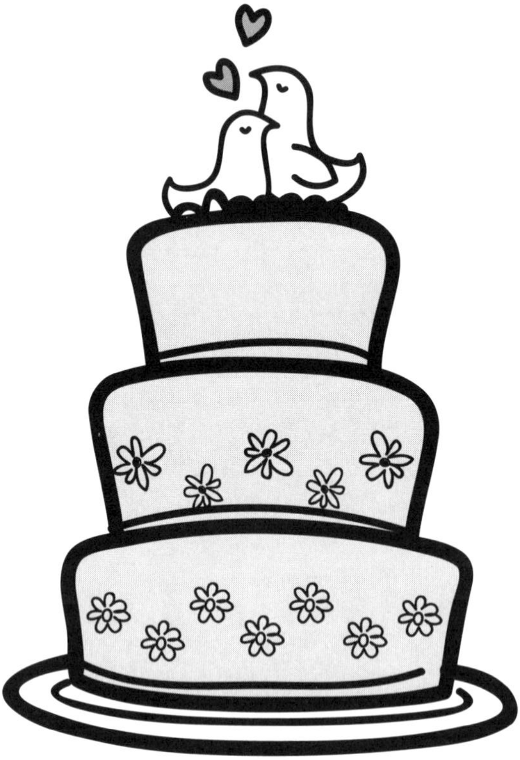

8. Cakes

Cakes and desserts play an important role in the overall wedding process. Maybe you are too busy dancing to see them or taste them, but we guarantee they are present. Plan to spend about 2–3 percent of your wedding budget on cakes. You have many options to consider when deciding on a wedding cake or a special dessert at your reception. You'll need to choose dessert type, size, and bakery.

Most couples like to coordinate the cake to match their wedding theme or type. For example, you might want colors that reflect the bridesmaids' dresses or a design that mimics the details of the bride's dress. If you are planning a theme wedding, have the cake represent the theme. If you are having an old-fashioned Victorian theme, for example, have the cake decorated in lace.

Personalizing the cake is another fabulous idea. For instance, include your new initials on the cake, set your wedding cake on an antique plate that has been in your family for decades, or add a flavor that's reminiscent of a place you have traveled to together. For example, if your first trip together was to Hawaii, you could include coconut flavoring.

Another great idea is to honor an important friend or family member with a flavor or decoration. Perhaps your grandmother loved making lemon pies and your family had them every holiday; you could add lemon filling to part of the cake in honor of her. Remember, it's your cake; create what's significant to you.

Timeline

3 – 6 months
- Start searching and interviewing bakeries.
- For more popular bakeries, start a year in advance.

1 – 2 weeks
- Follow up with your bakery to finalize all details.

If you aren't a wedding cake kind of couple, don't feel like you have to have an elaborate cake. Many brides and grooms choose to have something besides a wedding cake. Most caterers offer dessert selections in addition to or in replacement of a cake. Some even offer dessert stations.

A few other creative ideas include individual cupcakes stacked and decorated differently, a chocolate fountain with all the fixings (see Chapter 13, "And Everything Else"), or a dessert that follows your ethnic background or a place that is special to the bride and groom. For instance, if you come from an Italian background, you could serve cannolis and tiramisu. Or if you have a Greek background, serve baklava. If your favorite place to go for a sweet treat is Krispy Kreme, opt for cake made of delicious doughnuts. Just because most people choose to have cakes, doesn't mean that your reception has to follow. Be creative!

👍 Do's & Don'ts 👎

- Interview and taste-test several bakeries before making your final decision.

- If you are considering a custom cake or dessert, bring photos to the interviews.

- For more noticeable placement, consider putting your cake in the middle of the dance floor or on the lobby table before serving.

- Provide cute to-go boxes for your guests to take a piece of wedding cake home.

💰 Money-Saving Tips

- Because cakes are usually priced by the slice, go for a smaller cake that is designed to perfection and have sheet cake in the same flavor. When the caterer brings the cake to the kitchen to cut it, he will use the sheet cake to serve guests, and no one will ever know.

- The caterer at the reception venue might include a cake in your price range or has a contract with a neighborhood baker who can offer a discount.

- If a close friend or a family member makes cakes for a living or for a hobby, ask for that as your wedding gift and cut costs significantly.

- Choose cheaper ingredients, especially for the icing. Fondant can be much pricier than traditional buttercream.

- Opt for a plain cake with fewer designs and dress it up with fresh flowers or fresh fruit.

- Borrow cake-cutting knives or toppers from friends or family.

The Cakery

1420 Tamm Avenue | St. Louis, Missouri 63139
314 647 6000
www.thecakerybakery.net
Cost: Starts at $3.00 a person

The Cakery's cake studio and bakery located in Dogtown is owned by two young ladies, Ericka and Julie. Ericka has been creating cakes and desserts for more than 20 years. She started the Cakery out of her home, and in 2004, she partnered with Julie to open the storefront. The Cakery has been featured many times in local media for their outstanding work. Their wedding cakes range in colors, unique designs, and flavors. Want to match your cake with your bridesmaid dresses or your color scheme? These ladies can do it! Take a look at the cake gallery online to get a feel for what types of cakes they can master.

Carondelet Bakery

7726 Virginia Avenue | St. Louis, Missouri 63111
314 638 3519
www.carondeletbakery.com
Cost: Call for pricing

If you are a St. Louis history buff, you know that this is St. Louis' oldest bakery. Still in the original building, Carondelet Bakery has been in business since 1875, and today the owners, Bob and Linda Smith, operate it and live upstairs. Bob started working there when he was 13 years old, sweeping floors, and just look at him today! Linda decorates every cake, and she enjoys meeting with each bride and groom to discover their needs and wants. The bakery sells more than 250 cakes a year. Stop by and see why the Carondelet Bakery is still as popular today as it was more than 125 years ago.

Hank's Cheesecakes

1063 South Big Bend | St. Louis, Missouri 63117
314 781 0300
www.hankscheesecakes.com
Cost: Call for pricing

Who doesn't like cheesecake? Imagine having one designed for your wedding cake. Hank's Cheesecakes is the perfect place for both cheesecakes and beautiful wedding cakes. If you have seen the work they do, you know exactly what we're talking about. Hank's has been in business since 1983 and is famous around town for the fabulous cheesecakes. Their wedding cheesecakes come in a wide range of styles and flavors. Believe us, you and your guests won't be disappointed!

Heaven Scent Bakery

1133 Bryan Road | O'Fallon, Missouri 63366
636 332 6435
www.heavenscentbakery.com
Cost: Call for pricing

Starting as just a little donut shop in O'Fallon, Missouri, in 1995, Heaven Scent Bakery has come a long way in just over 14 years. They are now offering everything from a basic cake donut to wedding invitations and bridal party gifts. If you visit their wedding showroom and don't see a wedding cake design that fits your needs, don't worry because they will create one just for you! You can even bring a picture of your dream cake and they can duplicate it. That means you and your guests are not limited to any color, shape, or size. Now that's what we call service!

Knodel's Bakery

6621 W. Florissant | St. Louis, Missouri 63136
314 385 2000
2127 Barrett Station Road | Town and Country, Missouri 63131
314 822 5151
www.knodelsbakery.com
Cost: Call for pricing

Knodel's is yet another famous bakery known to many St. Louisans as well as others across the United States. Karl Knodel opened his bakery in 1901 focusing on wedding and special occasion cakes. Handing the company down from family member to family member, today all the cakes are designed by Karl's great-granddaughter, Cynthia Winders, keeping the family tradition significant. The Knodel's family believes that wedding cakes have three parts: structure, style, and taste. With decades of proficiency, each cake is designed specially for the wedding couple's preference.

Lubeley's Bakery

7815 Watson Road | St. Louis, Missouri 63119
314 961 7160
www.lubeleysbakery.com
Cost: Call for pricing

Founded in 1937, Lubeley's is a well-recognized family-owned and operated bakery located in South St. Louis. They concentrate on customizing your wedding cake to fit your style and needs, whether it is traditional or unique. Lubeley's has many cake flavors, fillings, and icing flavors to choose from. Take a look online for pictures of wedding cakes they offer, or stop by their store to look at hundreds of cakes they have on display in albums. We promise you won't be disappointed and your guests will be taking more than one piece! Lubeley's recommends ordering your cake six months prior to the big day.

McArthur's Bakery

3055 Lemay Ferry Road | St. Louis, Missouri 63125
314 894 0900
www.mcarthurs.com
Cost: Starts around $2.40 per person

At one time or another you have probably heard this famous St. Louis bakery's name come up in conversation. Because they have been in business for more than 40 years, whether it's a magical kid's birthday cake or a beautiful anniversary cake of your grandparents, someone you know has used them. When deciding on a bakery for Emily's wedding, McArthur's was the first name that popped into her head. And of course, it turned out delicious. They have more than a handful of artists specially designated for wedding cakes, and they have every flavor you can imagine.

The main location of McArthur's, on Lemay Ferry Road, has a wedding showroom where you can view photo albums and slideshows and shop for accessories for your special day. Call and make an appointment for a wedding consultation to taste and design your cake.

Sugaree Baking Company

1242 Tamm Avenue | St. Louis, Missouri 63139
314 645 5496
www.sugareebaking.com
Cost: Call for pricing

Sugaree Baking Company is a great neighborhood bakery located in historic Dogtown that designs some of the most unique wedding cakes we have seen. It is owned by Pat Rutherford-Pettine and her husband, Jim, who have years of culinary expertise. Originally, Pat was the pastry chef at a famous catering company in St. Louis, but she decided to branch off and use her skills further. When things got busy, Jim joined her and the rest is history. The cakes' distinctive appeal and taste are to die for. (The carrot cake in particular is fabulous, by the way!)

Truffes, Inc.

622 N. Skinker Boulevard | St. Louis, Missouri 63130
314 863 6347
www.gooeychocolate.com
Cost: Call for pricing

Truffes was started in 1987 by Helen S. Fletcher and today it is one of the most appreciated specialty bakeries in St. Louis. Truffes began as a mail-order cookie service where you could order holiday cookies by the tin; today it has evolved into making specialty desserts for local restaurants, hotels, and caterers serving hundreds of people. Their products can even be found in select Schnuck's and Straub's supermarkets. They offer many unique cake fillings, such as Lemon Mist, Raspberry Waltz, and Hazelnut Dream, to name a few. If you are interested in a more basic cake, they can whip that up for you, too!

Wedding Wonderland

449 Dunn Road | Florissant, Missouri 63031
314 837 5015
www.weddingwonderlandcakes.com
Cost: Starts at $1.55 a serving

If you are looking for something artistic, Wedding Wonderland might just be the bakery for you. This award-winning bakery was referred by *Ace of Cakes*' Charm City Bakery. Located in North County, Wedding Wonderland has been operating for more than 20 years. With perhaps the largest selection in St. Louis, you can either choose one of their samples or create one of your own. Wedding Wonderland concentrates on one thing only—cakes!

Questions to Ask Your Cake Designer

- Do you have a portfolio/picture gallery of the wedding cakes you have designed in the past?
- Can we have a tasting of the different kinds of wedding cakes and fillings?
- Is an appointment or wedding cake consultation appointment required for a tasting?
- Are there set designs we have to choose from, or will you custom design a cake if we provide a picture or drawing?
- How do you price your cakes? By the serving or slice? Is there an extra charge for fillings? If we want a more complicated design, is there an extra charge? Do you have a price list?
- Do you have or can we rent stands, cake toppers, tiers, and cutters? How much extra are those?
- If we choose fresh flowers, will you coordinate with my florist, will you provide them, or will we need to get the flowers to you?
- Do you provide groom's cakes?
- What type of ingredients go into making the cakes, filling, and icing?
- How far in advance are the cakes prepared? How long will it take to prepare the cake? (The closer to your wedding that the cake is made, the better it will taste.)
- How many cakes does this bakery do per weekend? (This will tell you how much effort that they will put into each cake.)
- Do you deliver? What is the delivery charge? Will the person who is delivering it set up for us or do we need to coordinate the setup ourselves?
- Can you provide references?

Notes

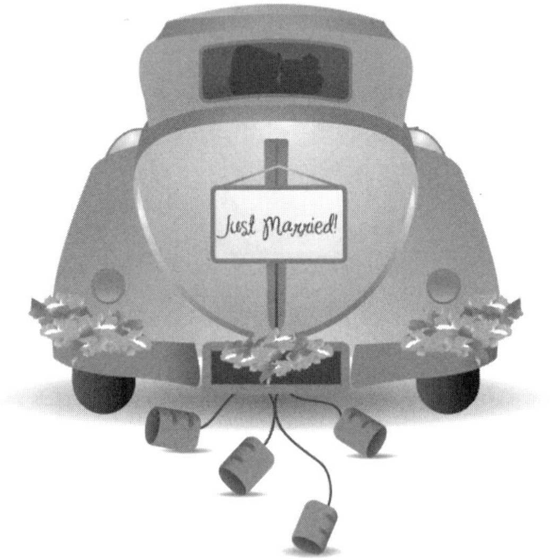
Just Married!

9. Transportation

This chapter is near and dear to Allison because she has a bit of a horror story. Since Allison's entire wedding was the traditional church wedding and hotel reception, she wanted the classic Rolls-Royce limousine to go with it. Two weeks before the wedding when she called to confirm her reservation, the company told her the specific limo she reserved was no longer available and she would have to have a normal stretch limousine! Because of her budget she couldn't upgrade, and with it being two weeks before her wedding, there was no time to get that specific car from another company. Her hands were tied and she was stuck with something she didn't want. Moral of the story: be sure to ask what type of backup vehicle is available in case of emergency.

When choosing transportation for your wedding day you'll want to consider the time of year of your wedding, number of passengers, location of service in relation to your wedding venue (they may charge for travel time if they are too far), type of transportation, and of course budget. Before you make a decision, take into account your needs as well as the theme or style of your wedding.

For example, a horse and buggy fits well for a rural outdoor wedding. But if you're into big and bold, a stretch Hummer may be more your style. Think about your profession, hobby, or theme of your wedding for a fun and unique transportation idea, such as a school bus, fire truck, police car, 18-wheeler, tractor, golf cart, bicycle, snowmobile, motorcycle, classic or antique car, horseback, horse and carriage, horse and wagon, hot air balloon... or for the gothic brides, a hearse. Also consider arranging transportation for your out-of-town guests to the rehearsal dinner, wedding, and/or reception. Rates fluctuate depending on day, season, and type of vehicle; we have listed average price ranges for Saturday night during peak season (April–October).

Timeline

6 – 9 months
- Interview and choose transportation.

1 month
- Arrange transportation for out-of-town guests.
- Finalize and confirm details for all transportation.

1 – 2 weeks
- Make final confirmation for transportation.

Do's & Don'ts

- Begin by narrowing your list to two or three companies that fit your style and calling for an appointment.
- Consider the season of your wedding before deciding on your transportation. You may decide to skip the open carriage if you are getting married in December.
- Figure out the number of vehicles you will need and the number of passengers you will have per vehicle.
- To add flair to your wedding, consider unconventional means of transportation.
- Horse-drawn vehicles are available for all size parties and all seasons.
- Check which backup vehicles are available in case of emergency!

Money-Saving Tips

- Limo prices are higher in the spring because of prom season, and you'll need to book one year ahead versus the usual six months for that time of year.
- Weekdays (including Fridays) are less expensive than weekends.
- Off-peak season (usually November to March) is less expensive than peak.

Balloons Over St. Louis

12245 Rain Hollow Drive | St. Louis, Missouri 63043
314 434 4241
www.balloonsoverstl.com
Cost: $600 for two passengers

How about arriving at your wedding by hot air balloon? Hot air balloons fly at sunrise or two hours prior to sunset. Keep in mind that you'll need good weather and two and a half to three hours before your wedding for this. Flights usually take an hour to an hour and a half, but with preparation time you'll need approximately three hours. The balloons will hold two passengers plus the pilot. Balloons Over St. Louis has been open for 30 years, and the owners are both full-time hot air balloon pilots that have flown almost 4,000 hours. What a unique way to arrive at your wedding!

Brookdale Farms

8004 Twin Rivers Road | Eureka, Missouri 63025
636 938 1005
www.brookdalefarmsinc.com
Cost: Call for pricing

This reputable company services the Riverfront with Carriage rides and offers several types of horse-drawn vehicles for your event. Brookdale Farms offers services year-round, and many of the drivers have been working there for years. They offer horse-drawn vehicles for all size wedding parties, all seasons, and all styles. The Vis-à-Vis seats up to six people. For larger parties, the Trolleys seat up to 35 passengers. For a Western-themed wedding try a Stage Coach that seats up to nine folks. Go dashing through the snow of your winter wedding with a horse-drawn Sleigh for up to four friends or family members. For larger parties try the refurbished Hotel Coach or Wagonette, which seats 16-18 passengers. The Hotel Coach seats up to 16 and has windows in case of inclement weather. Large or small, snow or shine, rural or urban—Brookdale Farms has a horse-drawn vehicle that will work for you.

Central States Trailways

11774 Missouri Bottom Road | St. Louis Missouri 63042 | 314 731 4324
www.centralstatestrailways.com
Cost: $85 to $150/hour plus $100 cleaning fee (4-hour minimum)

Central States Trailways offers a wide range of Coaches seating 23–55 passengers. They have a variety of Trolleys, Coaches, and Buses to choose from. One of our favorites is the classic red and green Trolley that holds up to 36 guests with open-air or air-conditioning capability. For a more cozy option, the various Coaches hold from 23 to 55 passengers with TV/VCR/DVD, air conditioning, and restrooms available.

Country Club Limousine

5140 N. Service Road | St. Peters, Missouri 63376 | 636 928 LIMO
www.countryclublimos.com
Cost: $65/hour to $350/hour (4-hour minimum)

If you have your heart set on a Hummer, check out the selection at Country Club Limousines. They have several Hummers available, including those nicknamed "Ice," "X-Factor," and "High Roller" because of their unique features. Besides Hummers (seat 23–25), they also offer Chrysler 300s (seat 8–9), Lincoln Towncars (seat 8–9), Limo Bus (seats 14–25), and Party Shuttle (seats up to 16).

Perfect Touch Limousines

P.O. Box 349 | Hazelwood, Missouri 63042 | 314 731 LIMO
www.aperfecttouchlimo.com
Cost: $65/hour to $275/hour (3-hour minimum)

This family-owned business, open since 1992, offers nice, affordable vehicles including stretch limos (seat 6–14), Jaguar S Type (seats up to 10), Chrysler 300 (seats up to 12), Cadillac Escalade (seats 14–18), and Luxury Coaches (seat 18–38). (Rated Top Pick by Local St. Louis area brides on TheKnot.com for 2007, 2008 & 2009!)

Rogers' Limousine

40 Jefferson Square | Desoto, Missouri 63050
636 337 0119
www.rogerslimo.com
Cost: $75 to $325/hour (4-hour minimum)

This family-owned business of 13 years offers newer, clean vehicles with dependable drivers. They have several limousines and coaches to choose from including a Lincoln Towncar, a 10-passenger Chrysler 300C, a 12-passenger Lincoln Navigator, a 16-passenger Escalade, and 26- to 40-passenger coaches. Limo rates depend on the type and size of vehicle and the day of the week. Special rates are available for six-, eight-, or ten-hour rentals.

St. Louis Carriage Company

1000 Cerre | St. Louis, Missouri 63102
314 621 3334
www.stlouiscarriagecompany.com
Cost: Horse-Drawn: $275 first hour, $100 each additional hour
Limo & Coach: $325 to $500 first hour, $100 each additional hour
Hearse: Call for pricing
Hay Wagon: $400 first hour, $100 each additional hour

Serving St. Louis for more than 20 years, not only does St. Louis Carriage Company specialize in beautiful horse-drawn vehicles but they are also the only company in St. Louis familiar with weddings that have a Hearse available for rent. Horse-drawn vehicles include a Vis-à-Vis and Landau (seat up to 6), Limo (seats up to 10), Hotel Coach or Trolley (seats up to 26), and Hay Wagon (seats up to 20). They have a variety of interior colors to choose from for several of the vehicles.

Questions to Ask Your Transportation Provider

- Is the vehicle we want available for our date and times?
- What are the model, make, year, size, and colors of the vehicles we are renting?
- How long have you been in business?
- How many drivers do you have?
- If we decide to book, may we have the driver's name and phone number?
- Will someone be on-site at your facility the day of my wedding in case of questions or emergency? If not, what is the name and number of whom I can contact that day?
- How many years of experience do your drivers have?
- May I see a list of your testimonials or references?
- Does your company carry liability insurance?
- Tell me about your licensing and operating authority. (They are required to have federal and state operating authority.)
- Are you affiliated with the Better Business Bureau, National Limousine Association, Livery Association, or Chamber of Commerce?
- What is your payment/cancellation policy?
- Do you offer special rates or discounts for different days of the week? Combination packages?
- What is included in the price? Do you offer specials for weddings such as champagne toast, flowers or other décor, signs, photos, interior color changes, etc.?
- What is the starting time for our rental? (Usually it's time of pickup.)
- Do you charge travel time if you are too far from me?
- Do you charge overtime?
- What gratuity do you charge? (It's usually 15–20 percent.)
- Upon hiring you, will I receive a detailed contract? What does that generally cover? Can you guarantee make, model, and color of vehicle?

Notes

10. Stationery

As the first items your guests will see, your invitations set the tone of your wedding. You have several choices to make including the types of stationery you'll need, the style, and where to buy them. We'll give you the basics and some background on our favorites so you can make an informed, hassle-free decision.

There is a plethora of wedding stationery available. Most couples mail invitations, reception cards, and response cards, and have programs available at the ceremony. Other popular stationery are save-the-date cards or magnets that may include travel and hotel information. Another popular choice is including with the invitation a map with directions and your wedding website with registry information. Other fun options to coordinate with invitations include menu cards, place cards, rain cards (plan B for outdoor locations), pew cards (assigned ceremony seating), favor tags, napkins, and thank-you cards. After the wedding, consider wedding announcements or "just moved" cards with your new name, address, and phone number.

Finally, you have five options for purchase. Seemingly most affordable is to create your own. This is very time-consuming, especially if you aren't a whiz on the computer, but you have total control over your design and can show off your originality. Printing your own invitations can get expensive depending on where you go and how many you need, so this may not end up saving you money in the long run, but there are computer programs you can buy to help you.

Buying online has the fastest turnaround time. You can order when it's convenient for you and easily shop around for the best price. But just like any other item purchased online, what you get may not always be what you expected. Color, size, and texture could be distorted when viewing on the computer. Also, be sure to carefully proofread everything before you purchase.

Timeline

9 – 12 months
- Mail the Save-the-Date cards.

6 – 9 months
- Interview stationer and order your stationery.

3 – 6 months
- Mail invitations.

1 month
- Make table, menu, and place cards if needed.
- Call any guests that haven't responded.

Stationery stores are the most common way to purchase your stationery. It's affordable because you order straight from a catalog, and they have so many customers they can keep prices low. The drawback is you're not getting anything customized or original. But with all of the cute options and various brands to choose from, it isn't likely that someone you know will choose the exact same invitation.

Independent stationers are a great option if you are looking for customized invitations and individualized service. But you are going to pay for what you get. If uniqueness is worth the extra cost to you, then this is a great way to go.

For the utmost in originality and creativity use a graphic designer. Emily used some designer friends of ours and her stationery turned out really cool and customized for an affordable price. A drawback to graphic designers is that you have to pay the designer plus a printer. Depending on the designer's fees and the print quality you're looking for, this could get expensive. Presented in this chapter are some of our favorite graphic designers, independent stationers, stationery stores, and calligraphers in town.

Do's & Don'ts

- Send one invitation per household.

- Check etiquette for wording of invitations and addressing the envelopes, particularly if you are creating your own.

- Be sure to mail out all your invitations at the same time to avoid hurt feelings.

- For a creative and unique idea; name place cards after each of the dorms you lived in during college, streets you lived on as a kid, and teams that you played for.

- Choose a photo, graphic, font, color, or monogram and carry it throughout all of your stationery. This will give everything a unified look.

Money-Saving Tips

- Use only one color of ink, or for even more savings cut out colored ink altogether and use black.

- Use a reply postcard instead of a card with envelope to save on postage.

- Use thermography instead of engraving, the traditional type of printing. Thermography is half the cost.

- Beware of thicker, oversized, odd-shaped, square, charmed, and ribboned invitations because of the cost of postage.

- Check with your groom's attire store for discounts on invitations if you order from them.

- Weigh a complete invitation at the post office for exact postage needed. This will save you expensive returned invitations or mismatched stamps from adding extra postage.

- Check out computer programs available for "do-it-yourself" stationery.

Anda Creative

P.O. Box 21743 | St. Louis, MO 63109
314 397 1471
www.andacreative.com
Cost: Call for pricing

Amanda Potts and Miranda Summers are the owners and designers at Anda Creative. They are friends of ours and made really cool, original invitations and maps for Emily's wedding at a better price than she could find at stationery stores. Personally, they are both really easygoing but detail oriented and fun to work with. They have both been in design since they graduated from Mizzou and Truman State University, respectively, in 1998. They also designed our company logo, so if you like the style, check them out for your wedding.

Barbara Winnerman Calligraphy

416 Conway Wold Byway | St. Louis, Missouri 63141
314 434 3478
http://home.earthlink.net/~bawinnie/
Cost: $0.60 to $0.70 per line

Barbara Winnerman's occupation has been calligraphy for 30 years and her exquisite work and creativity reflect that experience. Besides her six standard envelope styles she also creates custom fonts for your invitations, programs, menus, and table and place cards. Her custom fairytale-like calligraphy is so beautiful and unique, unlike any we could find in town.

Crane & Co. Paper Makers

52 Plaza Frontenac | St. Louis, Missouri 63131
314 994 1300
www.crane.com
Cost: $191 and up for 50 invitations

Crane & Co. has 18 retail locations nationwide with all of their invitations made and designed by Crane. They offer a personalized wedding collection that not only allows you to choose the type and ink color but also the paper, lettering style, motif, and envelope lining for a more custom invitation. Shop online for your convenience.

D & D Designs

314 283 1491
www.dddesignsonline.com
Cost: Call for pricing

For simple, elegant custom invitations talk to Kimberly, owner and designer at D & D Designs. She creates original works tailored to your wedding style. Designing stationery since 1996, her work is now available nationwide. As an added feature, all invitations come assembled for no additional cost. Consultation by appointment.

Stationery

The Event Messenger

214 734 8095
www.theeventmessenger.com
Cost: Call for pricing

For high quality, contemporary, fully coordinated custom stationery with an environmentally friendly focus, The Event Messenger will work great for you. The Event Messenger uses mostly recycled paper, biodegradable packing materials, and paper vendors with a green focus. Soy or vegetable-based ink is available for additional cost. They also use electronic samples (although paper swatch books are available), proofs, and invoicing. Carrie Foiles, owner and designer of The Event Messenger and originally a St. Louis native, recently relocated to Dallas. Allison and Carrie have been friends since they were in diapers and even as a child Carrie was a creative, artistic little girl. Allison used her for baby Adam's announcements and was more than impressed with her work. The texture and color of the electronic proofs looked exactly like the actual announcements she received. Carrie designs precious keepsakes that will last a lifetime.

The Stationery Lady Invitations

12555 Mason Forest Drive | St. Louis, Missouri 63141
314 514 9589
www.stationerylady.invitations.com
Cost: Call for pricing

Order your invitations using a large selection of vendors from Sally Kaplan, owner of The Stationery Lady Invitations. She offers affordable stationery services available online or in-store, including custom invitations. She has an enormous selection of catalogs on hand, such as Birchcraft, Checkerboard, Elite, Embossed Graphics, Encore, Regency and more. Specials include free shipping for orders over $500.

Two Blue Doors

7 Gray Avenue | Webster Groves, Missouri 63119
314 968 4033
www.twobluedoors.com
Cost: Call for pricing

From sophisticated, delicate, panel cards to modern, bold, accordion-fold invitations, Beth and Elizabeth, co-owners of Two Blue Doors, have something original and creative up their sleeves to make your invitations unique and beautiful. From invitations to maps, they custom design stationery with creativity of shape, color, and style not matched by other stationers in town. Call for an appointment. They also offer calligraphy services.

Vellum

120 West Monroe | St. Louis, Missouri 63122
314 909 1640
www.velluminc.com
Cost: Call for pricing

Open since 2002, this Kirkwood stationer has been called the "sassiest stationery store in town" by *Where St. Louis*. They have also been featured in *St. Louis At Home Magazine*, and *St. Louis Magazine*. Owners Kerri Williamson, Kippin Sanchez, and Julie Redmond have professional backgrounds in marketing and journalism. From conventional to modern, they have a large selection of vendors to choose from to complement your wedding style or theme. At Vellum, their goal is to make shopping for invitations and stationery fun and affordable. Rush shipping and delivery are available at additional charge.

Questions to Ask Your Stationer

- Are you a catalog or custom stationer?
- How long have you been in business?
- How long once we order until we receive our invitations?
- What is your guarantee if there is a mistake?
- How much do we pay upon ordering?
- Will you print the envelopes, too, and for what price?
- Do you offer a proof to check setup and typestyle? (Most will give you a black and white proof for a small fee.)

For Calligraphers

- How long have you been doing calligraphy for wedding invitations?
- How much do you charge?
  Do you charge by the set or per line?
- What styles do you offer? Will you do a custom style?
- Can you match my invitation font to the envelope font?
- Do you charge for redoing mistakes?
- Will you stamp, seal, and stuff the invitations? Is there an additional fee for this service? (Some companies will even mail them for you.)
- How many extra envelopes will we need, if any?
- May I have a list of references?
- Do I need to sign a contract?

Notes

122 Dresses

11. Dresses

The bride's dress is a key symbol of a wedding. Little girls imagine wearing their dress years before they meet a groom. Besides the bride and groom, the dress is another main focus of the wedding that will be captured in photos for years to come. Bridal attire accounts for 5-10 percent of your budget and includes dress, shoes, veil and/or headpiece, lingerie, jewelry, and alterations.

Bring to your appointments

- Pictures of ideas from magazines or web sites
- Shoes with heel the same size you'll wear on your wedding day
- Budget
- One or two friends or family
- Camera—check with boutique first, though; some won't allow them
- Strapless bra similar to what you'll wear on your wedding day

7 Do's & 7 Don'ts

- Have a good idea of what you're looking for before you shop.
- Keep an open mind toward salespeople's suggestions.
- Best time to shop is during a weekday. Saturdays are extremely busy.
- To save time, check online and call ahead to be sure what you are looking for is in stock to try on.
- Put everything on a credit card so you are protected.
- "Sleep on it" for a night before you buy.

Timeline

9 - 12 months
- Schedule bridal attire appointments and visit at least three bridal stores.

6 - 9 months
- Order bridal gown.
- Decide on bridesmaids' dresses and order.

2 months
- Schedule the first dress fitting.

1 month
- Schedule last dress fitting and possible pickup.

Money-Saving Tips

- If you find your dress at a more expensive boutique, check around. You may be able to find the exact same dress at a less expensive store like David's Bridal or online.
- Don't limit yourself to bridal shops. Check for sales at department stores such as Saks Fifth Avenue's Bridal Suite.
- Check with your store to see if they offer discounts for buying the bridal gown and bridesmaid dresses at the same store.
- Try buying "try-on" models during winter or summer sales. They usually come in size 8 or 10, so if you're those sizes you'll have more luck. The dress will need to be cleaned but the savings might outweigh the cost of the cleaning.
- Try buying floor models.
- Try consignment shops.
- Avoid hand-sewn beading or lacework.
- Avoid lots of fabric versus a simple silhouette.
- Avoid custom alterations such as a changed neckline.

Bonnie's Formal Fashions

1001 S. Lincoln | O'Fallon, Illinois 62269
618 624 3611
www.bonniesformalfashions.com
Cost: Wedding gowns – $99 and up

Bonnie's Formal Fashions is a one-stop bridal shop including everything from bridal gowns to shoes. They have a wide range of designers to choose from, and they do their own fittings and alterations. They offer sizes 0 to 32 and up and no appointment is needed. Bonnie's also has a "Bargain Room" with discounted dresses and a "Consignment Corner" for all of those on a budget. They are open seven days a week and no appointment is needed. (Some places require an appointment just to try on a dress.)

Callahan's Tuxedo and Bridal Rental Company

3714 Gravois | St. Louis, Missouri 63116
8700 Gravois | Affton, Missouri 63123
314 664 5521
www.callahantuxedo.com
Cost: Wedding gowns – $99 to $400
Rental gowns – $200 to $300

For a more affordable option, Callahan's offers new, once worn, and rental bridal gowns. Located in south city on Gravois just west of South Grand, they also sell and rent bridesmaid gowns, flower girl dresses, tuxedos, headpieces, shoes, and accessories. Services they provide include gown preservation as well as discounts on Carlson Craft invitations and tuxedo rental. Since you only wear your dress once anyway, check them out for a more economical option.

Clarice's Bridal

4627 Hampton Avenue | St. Louis, Missouri 63109
314 351 2499
www.claricesbridal.com
Cost: Wedding gowns – $250 to $1,500

This third-generation family-owned bridal shop open since 1979 offers selections from more than seven designers, including Alfred Angelo, Demetrios, Jasmine, Maggie Sottero, and more. The quaint south city boutique also sells bridesmaid gowns, mother of the bride gowns, veils and headpieces, shoes, and accessories. Average sizes they carry to try on range from 6 to 16. This is where Emily found the bridesmaid dresses for her wedding, and she had a great experience with them. Special discounts are offered each month. Call for a professional, friendly appointment.

David's Bridal

10760 Sunset Hills Plaza | St. Louis, Missouri 63127
    314 909 8828 or 314 835 9066
5858 Suemandy Road | St. Peters, Missouri 63376
    636 279 9055 or 636 279 9035
14 Plaza Drive | MarketPlace Center | Fairview Heights, Illinois 62208
    618 394 0100 or 618 394 9107
www.davidsbridal.com
Cost: Wedding gowns – $99 to $1,450

David's Bridal is a bridal retailer with more than 280 locations nationwide. They offer dresses from their own designers, such as Monique Luo, Oleg Cassini, and Galina, which allows them to keep their prices affordable. They can order sizes 0 to 18 and 14W to 26W. Services include on-site alterations, dyeing, and discounts on gown preservation, invitations, and more. Besides bridal gowns, they carry bridesmaid gowns, flower girl dresses, mother of the bride dresses, veils and headpieces, shoes, and accessories. Allison bought her wedding dress here because she wanted an affordable dress, wasn't hung up on labels, and liked the convenient hours (they're open until 7:00 p.m. Saturday, 6:00 p.m. on Sunday, and 9:00 p.m. weekdays). Appointments preferred.

Elite/Bluestein's Brides House

1116 Wolfrum Road | St. Charles, Missouri 63304
636 447 8828
www.elitebridal.com
Cost: Call for pricing

Elite/Bluestein's Brides House is a family-owned business that opened in 1918. Emily purchased her wedding dress from Bluestien's when their location was downtown. Now located in Weldon Springs, they recently closed their downtown store and combined it with their other store in St. Peters to provide a full array of merchandise and services for all brides. Emily was very pleased with the service she received and would highly recommend them to any bride-to-be. They carry more than 50 designers' wedding gowns and also have bridesmaid dresses, mother's gowns, flower girl dresses, and much more. Call or stop by. Open six days a week.

Maiden Voyage Bridal

120 Henry Avenue | Manchester, Missouri 63011
636 394 5858
www.maidenvoyagebridal.com
Cost: Wedding gowns – $700 to $5,000

Located near I-270 and Manchester, this bridal salon offers more than 13 designers including Lazaro, Jim Hjelm, Anne Barge, Marissa Collection, Maggie Sottero, and Alfred Sung. They also carry bridesmaid gowns, flower girl dresses, mother of the bride dresses, and accessories. They offer in-store alterations and are open five days a week (closed Sunday and Tuesday). Call for an appointment.

Check out **www.beau-coup.com** for unique favors for bridal showers and weddings. They also offer personalized bridesmaid and groomsmen gifts and much more.

Sydney's Closet

11840 Dorsett Road | Maryland Heights, Missouri 63043
314 344 5066
www.sydneyscloset.com
Cost: Wedding gowns – $99 to $899

Most of us aren't built like supermodels, right? In fact, according to Phyllis Brasch Librach, founder of Sydney's Closet, 6 out of 10 Americans wear a size 12 or larger. She started this company for her teenage daughter who was having a hard time finding a plus-size dress for her high school dance. Now she also carries a variety of bridal gowns (sizes 14–44), bridesmaid gowns (sizes 0–44), and mother of the bride gowns. Sydney's Closet has been featured in *Teen*, *Twist*, and *Cosmo Girl* magazines as well as *ElleGirl.com* and *Seventeen.com* as a great source for plus-size formalwear. Although most orders are online, you can call for an appointment and she will open her showroom to you.

Town & Country Bridal Boutique

279 Lamp & Lantern Village | Town and Country, Missouri 63017
636 391 7700
www.townandcountrybride.com
Cost: Call for pricing

Located near Highway 141 and Clayton Road, this bridal boutique offers some posh designers including Justin Alexander, Modern Trousseau, Vineyard Collection, and Wtoo. They carry sizes 6 to 14 to try on but can order sizes 2 to 20 and up. Fittings and alterations are handled at the boutique. They also carry bridesmaid gowns, flower girl dresses, mother of the bride dresses, and accessories. Call for an appointment. Closed Sunday and Monday.

The Ultimate Bride

1512 S. Brentwood Boulevard | St. Louis, Missouri 63144
314 961 9997
www.theultimatebride.com
Cost: Call for pricing

Voted Best St. Louis Bridal Salon, according to their website, the Ultimate Bride boutique located near Highway 40 and Brentwood Boulevard offers many modish designers including Jim Hjelm, Romona Keveza, Lazaro, Monique Lhuillier, Marisa Collection, and Watters & Watters. They can order sizes 2 to 24 depending on the designer. They also carry bridesmaid gowns, flower girl dresses, headpieces, shoes, and accessories. Call for appointment only, Tuesday through Saturday. Open Sunday January through March.

Questions to Ask Your Bridal Boutique

Shop online first, then call to find out:

- What dresses, designers, and sizes do you have to try on?
- If you don't have the dress in stock I'm interested in, can you order it for me to try?
- What is the price of the dress I'm interested in?
- Does it come in my size (most dresses come in sizes 2–20)?
- Are you having a trunk show for this designer soon?
- What are your hours?
- Do I need an appointment?

Once you've decided on a dress:

- Does it having a matching headpiece or accessories?
- Can it be ordered with different train, neckline, or sleeves? What is the price difference? If I want to change these once it arrives, how much will that cost?
- What other colors does it come in (white, ivory)?
- How long will it take to come in once ordered?
- Will it look exactly like the dress I tried on?
- Do you do the alterations here? How much do they cost?
- Will I work with you again when I come in for fittings?
- Can I get a discount on my dress, bridesmaid dresses, or alterations for ordering bridesmaid dresses here as well?
- Do you offer discounts on any other of your products or services?
- What are your cancellation/refund policies?
- What is your payment policy?
- Does the contract or receipt list the designer's name, size, price, color, fabric, manufacturer, style number, and delivery date?

Notes

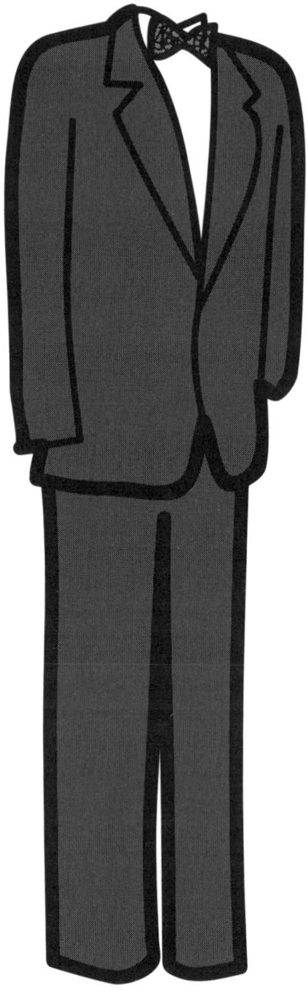

12. Tuxedos

Traditionally, most grooms wear a tuxedo for their wedding and in most cases, the same style as their attendants. To differentiate the groom from the others in the wedding party, he can wear, for example, a different jacket or a different color vest or bow tie. If you are planning something less formal, you might want to throw out the tux and settle for a dark suit. And if you are having a wedding that celebrates your ethnic heritage, such as a Scottish wedding, you may choose a kilt or other traditional attire. It's just a matter of taste and type of occasion.

Questions to Ask When Renting a Tux

- Are you offering any specials or discounts?
- Are alterations included in the price of the rental?
- Are the accessories (tie, shoes, cuff links, etc.) included in the price of the rental?
- How do you handle out-of-town groomsmen?
- What is the pickup and return policy?
- What are the late or damage fees?

Do's & Don'ts

Timeline

6 – 9 months
- Rent and reserve tuxedos for groom and wedding party.

1 month
- Finalize tuxedo alterations.

1 day
- Pick up and try on tuxes.

- Reserve all the tuxedos three to five months in advance.

- The tuxedo rental store should be able to provide all the accessories you will need: tie, cufflinks, suspenders, shoes, and so on.

- Have each groomsman get his attire at the same store to match perfectly. With ordering a number of other rentals, most stores will give the groom's tuxedo for free or at a discount.

- If your groomsmen live out of town, make sure they get measured by a local alteration shop or tailor and send the measurements to your shop.

Money-Saving Tips

- Wearing a dark suit that you already own will save you money, and the same goes for the groomsmen.

- It's more affordable to stick with a basic tux without a designer name.

- Avoid wedding dates around prom time. Tuxes are in high demand, which means higher prices.

- Some tuxedo rental stores offer wedding invitations at a discount with a certain number of tux rentals.

- Some bridal shops offer tuxedo rentals. If the bride is ordering her dress there, ask about discounts.

Callahan's Tuxedo

3714 Gravois | St. Louis, Missouri 63116
8700 Gravois | Affton, Missouri 63123
314 664 5521
www.callahanstuxedo.com
Cost: Rentals start at $65.00

Callahan's Tuxedo is family-owned and operated and has been in business for more than 45 years. They offer a wide variety of tuxedos, from classic to contemporary, to suit your style. Callahan's rents tuxedos by Chaps Ralph Lauren, Perry Ellis, Demetrios, Givenchy, Oscar De La Renta, and many other famous designers. In addition to tuxes, they also rent several styles of dress suits. If you have out-of-town guests in your wedding party, all they need to do is call in their measurements and Callahan's will have the tuxedo ready for pickup. Callahan's Tuxedo runs specials throughout the year, so make sure you ask for details, including a 25 percent discount on all invitations and favors.

Men's Wearhouse

10 locations around the St. Louis area
1 800 776 SUIT for a location near you
www.menswearhouse.com
Cost: Rentals start at $59.99

With more than 1,000 locations around the United States, 10 locations around the St. Louis area, and two in Illinois, Men's Wearhouse is a perfect choice for tuxedo rentals. Basic tuxedo rentals start at $59.99, and they offer a wide array of tuxedo styles by Joseph & Feiss, Jones of New York, Kenneth Cole Reaction, Calvin Klein, and Ralph Lauren. Men's Wearhouse offers many different specials, including one free tuxedo with four or more paid rentals within a wedding party. Other specials and discounts are offered on their website.

Savvi Formalwear

Eight locations around the St. Louis area
1 800 TUXEDO 4 for a location near you
www.savviwedding.com
Cost: Rentals start at $59.95

Savvi Formalwear, formerly Gingiss for 35 years, is family owned and operated. They have nine locations in the St. Louis area and three in Illinois. They have the latest styles with designer tuxedos from Calvin Klein, Perry Ellis, Ralph Lauren, and more. Red Sleeve, their exclusive designer, is fashionable, comfortable, and hip. Savvi also has many specials throughout the year to help save money for the couple.

Stallone's Formalwear

Six locations around the St. Louis area
1 800 666 5901 for a location nearest you
www.stallonesformalwear.com
Cost: Call for pricing

Stallone's Formalwear has been serving St. Louis since 1899. They offer top-quality tuxedos, and they have trained individuals who can help you every step of the way. Stallone's even offers custom ties: just bring in a piece of cloth from the bridesmaid dresses, and they will create a tie that coordinates with the dresses. If you have out-of-town guests, they can fill out a form online and Stallone's is happy to handle the rest. Stallone's also offers invitations, and if you book your wedding party with them, you will receive 30 percent off the invitation purchase.

Notes

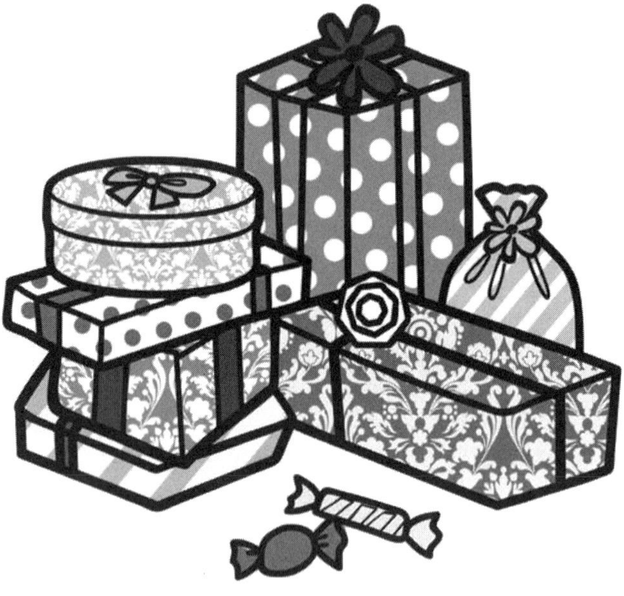

13. And Everything Else

Haven't seen anything out of the ordinary lately and just want to do something different for your wedding? What if you want to release butterflies or doves? Want fireworks or confetti? Want to have a photo booth for your guests to take pictures? Or St. Louis-themed gift baskets for out-of-town guests? This chapter is full of unique ideas and services around town for your guests, ceremony, and reception that we discovered through our research and could hardly wait to tell you about!

For your guests ...

St. Louis Gift Baskets

16514 Manchester Road | Wildwood, Missouri 63040
636 458 8359
www.stlouisgiftbaskets.com
Cost: $35 to $150

As welcome gifts for out-of-town guests St. Louis Gift Baskets, a woman-owned and -operated business for the past seven years, offers our favorite St. Louis-themed welcome baskets. Choose a basket that includes a map and guidebook for St. Louis; St. Louis products such as Fitz's root beer, beer, and wine; and sports and Arch-themed food items.

For your ceremony...

Amazing Butterflies

800 808 6276
www.amazingbutterflies.com
Cost: $65 to $95 per dozen

For summer weddings, imagine releasing dozens of butterflies at your ceremony, symbolizing transformation, beauty, freedom, and happiness. Have everyone at your ceremony release a butterfly, the wedding party only, or a basket of butterflies for the bride and groom. The only stipulations are that they are released at least 30 minutes before sunset in 62° F to 72° F (depending on the type) weather. Our friends Annique and Adam gave each guest a Monarch butterfly to release after their outdoor ceremony and it was so stunning to see hundreds of butterflies emerging from the gathering of wedding guests.

Show Me Doves

636 978 1675
www.showmedoves.com
Cost: $100 and up

Traditionally released during the ceremony to symbolize fidelity, good luck, love, peace, and prosperity, white doves can be an elegant addition to your wedding. You can release between 2 and 100 doves up to one hour before sunset. No worries about the doves being harmed because they are trained to return to their home in St. Peters.

For your reception...

Glazed and Confused

4595 Chestnut Park Plaza | St. Louis, Missouri 63129
314 892 8382
www.glazed-confused.com
Cost: Call for pricing, depends on piece

As a distinctive guest book alternative, have a platter fired and glazed with all of your wedding guests' signatures on it. Glazed and Confused will personalize your platter with the couple's name and wedding date. Place it at the reception for all of your guests to sign, and then return it for glazing and firing for a practical keepsake. There are a variety of platter shapes, sizes, and design options to choose from. Also, check out their private party room for showers and bachelorette parties.

Guestbookstore.com

www.guestbookstore.com
Cost: $24 and up

For a more personal guest book, check out the Guestbook Store. Although not a local company, the idea was so cute we had to include it. Each of your guests will receive their own page to fill out and return to you. You easily assemble the returned pages into a customized guest book. The company suggests having your guests fill out the pages while they are waiting for you to arrive at the reception. The book has room for 120–200 guest pages. Options include a variety of cover designs and material, casual or formal page styles, standard or photo page layouts, and customized page designs. For the photo page layout, attach a photo of each of your guests to each page. To make this option easier, couple this service with PhotoboothStL (Page 143) so you can order a photo of each of your guests online.

Ice Cuisine

1919 Geyer Avenue | St. Louis, Missouri 63104
314 865 4232
www.icecuisine.com
Cost: $215.00 for single block

Unique designs such as a royal carriage, Irish claddagh, and stained glass with doves make Ice Cuisine a great choice for your ice sculpture desires. They also create custom designs. Price includes sculpture and display tray, delivery, setup, and tray return. Sculptures generally last five to seven hours in 70° F temperatures.

Ice Visions

324 Sante Avenue | St. Louis, Missouri 63122
314 821 1204
www.icevisions.com
Cost: $249.00 for single block

Choose from hundreds of designs of ice sculptures for your wedding, or have a custom design. Some exclusive wedding designs include a castle, the Eiffel tower, a wine rack to chill and display wine, and a shrimp cake. The price includes the sculpture and display tray, delivery within 25 miles, setup, and tray return.

Photobooth STL

4406 Arsenal Street | St. Louis, Missouri 63116
314 776 3003
www.photoboothstl.com
Cost: Starting at $1,000 for a 4-hour event

How fun would it be to have a commercial photo booth for your guests to take free photos of themselves! Try this instead of or in addition to favors. Choose a retro digital photo booth for black-and-white or color photos ($1,000 for a four-hour event) or a vintage black-and-white photo booth ($1,600 for a five-hour event). Price includes setup, shutdown, and an on-site technician. The color photo booths are digital, providing a CD option for the bride and groom containing the pictures taken throughout the event and a website to order more prints. Only about an hour setup and an hour takedown time is needed.

Twilight Fire & Illusions

P.O. Box 39498 | St. Louis, Missouri 63139
314 776 1885
www.twilight-fire.com
Cost: $1,500 to $50,000

Why not go all out and add some pyrotechnics to your reception! Twilight Fire will take care of all the details of a fireworks display for you, providing the fireworks, equipment, transportation, setup, firing, and breakdown. They no longer need wide outdoor areas for these displays and can service small outdoor areas such as backyards and indoor areas. They can even choreograph the display to your song or put your names in a heart. How cute is that!

Chocolate fountains have been gaining in popularity around town over the past five years. We hadn't heard of them while researching our own weddings, but now they seem to be everywhere. Some reception venues include a chocolate fountain in the wedding packages. Here are a couple of our favorites:

Chocolate Fountain Affair

Chesterfield, Missouri 63017
636 230 6763
www.chocolatefountainaffair.com
Cost: $350 to $595 per fountain

Chocolate Fountain Affair offers milk, dark, or white chocolate fountains that are 25–35 inches tall serving 100–300 guests per fountain. Cost includes three hours of service plus an attendant, skewers, decorative table accents, delivery, setup, and breakdown. It takes about 45 minutes for setup. Not included in the price (typical for all chocolatiers) are the dipping items; these you'll want to get from your caterer or from Chocolate Fountain Affair for $2.00–$3.50 per guest. Dipping items include fruit, pretzels, graham crackers, cookies, marshmallows, and Rice Krispies Treats.

Kamy Chocolate Fountains

16648 Green Pines Drive | Wildwood, Missouri 63011
314 397 5287
www.kamyfountains.com
Cost: Call for pricing

Kamy Chocolate Fountains offers milk, dark, or white chocolate fountains serving 125–250 guests per fountain. Cost includes three hours of service plus an attendant, the skewers, delivery, setup, and cleanup. Some dipping suggestions include pineapple, strawberries, bananas, nuts, brownie bites, and pound cake bites.

Notes

the St. Louis Wedding Book

About Us

Emily Ayala and Allison Hockett were raised right here in St. Louis where they attended Lindbergh High School. After high school Allison enrolled at Truman State University, graduating with a B.A. in psychology, where she met her husband, Brian. Emily attended Missouri State University, graduating with a B.S. in finance, where she met her husband, Paulo. Allison resides in Eureka, Missouri, with her husband and three children, Grace, 6 years; Claire, 3 years; and Adam, 1 year. Emily resides in O'Fallon, Missouri, with her husband and little boy, Sam, 1 year old.

Resources at a Glance

Ceremony Sites

The Butterfly House 8
Carondolet Park 9
Church of the Open Word
    Garden Chapel 10
Eliot Chapel 11
Ethical Society of St. Louis 11
The Jewel Box 12
Kiener Plaza & Morton D. May
    Amphitheater 12
World's Fair Pavilion 13

Officiants

All Couples Married 15
Assisi Weddings 15

Receptions

Anheuser-Busch Center 21
Busch Stadium 21
Butterfly House 22
Chase Park Plaza 23
The City Museum 23
The Falls Reception
    and Conference Center 24
Favazza's Rose of the Hill 24
Hendri's 25
Holiday Inn Southwest 25
Kemoll's/Top of the Met 26
Le Chateau 26
Lemp Mansion 27
Mad Art Gallery 27
Magic House 28
Mahler Ballroom 28
Marriott West 29
Melting Pot 29
Missouri Botanical Garden 30
Missouri Historical Society
    and Museum 30
Morgan Street Brewery 31
Mount Pleasant Winery 31
Ninth Street Abbey
    (and Patty Long Catering) 32
Old Hickory Golf Club 32
Orlando Gardens 33
Powell Symphony Hall 34
Randall Gallery 35
St. Louis Science Center 35
St. Louis Zoo 36
Schlafly Tap Room 37
Spazio's 37
The Studio Inn at St. Albans 38
Sunset 44 Bistro
    and Banquet Center 38
Two Hearts Banquet
    and Conference Center 39
Windows Off Washington 40
Wildflower Loft 40
World's Fair Pavilion 41

Catering

Butler's Pantry 48
Catering St. Louis 48
Cuisine d'Art 49
Gregory's Creative Cuisine 49
Hendri's Banquets and Catering 50
LaChef & Co. 50
Patty Long Catering 51
Russo's Gourmet Catering 51

Music

The Chesterfield Quartet 58
Complete Music 59
Harp Inspirations 59
Jukebox Productions 60
Spectrum Band 61
TKO Deejays 61
The Ultraviolets 62

Photography

Artisan Photography 67
Chris Croy Photography 67
CLC Photography 68
Memories Are Forever 68
Nordmann Photography 69
Signature Studio 70

Snapshot Photography 70
St. Louis Color, Inc. 71
Susan Jackson Photography 72
T. Kratzer Photography 72
Trotter Photo 73
Warwick Photography 73

Videography

Complete Video 80
Kevin Harder Videography 80
Lifetime Media 80
New Directions Media 81
Nordmann Productions 81
Video Vantages 82

Flowers

Don DeFoe's Flowers 88
Elegant Celebrations 88
Fresh Art, LLC 89
Les Bouquets 89
Petals Galore 90
Sisters Flowers & Gifts 90

Cakes

The Cakery 96
Carondelet Bakery 96
Hank's Cheesecakes 97
Heaven Scent Bakery 97
Knodel's Bakery 98
Lubeley's Bakery 98
McArthur's Bakery 99
Sugaree Baking Company 100
Truffes, Inc. 100
Wedding Wonderland 101

Transportation

Balloons Over St. Louis 107
Brookdale Farms 107
Central States Trailways 108
Country Club Limousine 108
Perfect Touch Limousines 108
Rogers' Limousine 109
St. Louis Carriage Company 109

Stationery

Anda Creative 116
Barbara Winnerman Calligraphy 116
Crane & Co. Paper Makers 117
D & D Designs 117
The Event Messenger 118
The Stationery Lady Invitations 118
Two Blue Doors 119
Vellum 119

Dresses

Bonnie's Formal Fashions 125
Callahan's Tuxedo
    and Bridal Rental Company 125
Clarice's Bridal 126
David's Bridal 126
Elite/Bluestien's Brides House 127
Maiden Voyage Bridal 127
Sydney's Closet 128
Town & Country Bridal Boutique 128
The Ultimate Bride 129

Tuxedos

Callahan's Tuxedo 135
Men's Wearhouse 135
Savvi Formalwear 136
Stallone's Formalwear 136

And Everything Else

St. Louis Gift Baskets 139
Amazing Butterflies 140
Show Me Doves 140
Glazed and Confused 141
Guestbookstore.com 141
Ice Cuisine 142
Ice Visions 142
Photobooth STL 143
Twilight Fire & Illusions 143
Chocolate Fountain Affair 144
Kamy Chocolate Fountains 144

Thank You!

Thank you so much for purchasing *The St. Louis Wedding Book*. We hope this book helped you plan your ultimate St. Louis wedding. We would also love for you to be a part of helping future brides plan their weddings in upcoming editions, so please contact us with your unique St. Louis finds, ideas, fun wedding anecdotes, mishaps, or nightmares. We can't wait to hear them! We also welcome all of your questions, comments, and suggestions.

Emily Ayala and Allison Hockett
authors

WRIGHT PUBLICATIONS

Wright Publications
6311 Ronald Reagan Drive, Suite 175
Lake St. Louis, MO 63367

Website: www.stlweddingbook.com
Email us: info@stlweddingbook.com
Be a Fan on Facebook: stlweddingbook
Follow us on Twitter: @stlweddingbook